The Art of
Fly-casting for
Stillwater Trout

The Art of Fly-casting for Stillwater Trout

MICHAEL MARSHALL

STANLEY PAUL

London   Sydney   Auckland   Johannesburg

Stanley Paul & Co. Ltd
An imprint of the Random Century Group
20 Vauxhall Bridge Road, London SW1V 2SA

Random Century Australia (Pty) Ltd
20 Alfred Street, Milsons Point, Sydney 2061

Random Century New Zealand Limited
PO Box 40–086, Glenfield, Auckland 10

Random Century South Africa (Pty) Ltd
PO Box 337, Bergvlei 2012, South Africa

First published 1991

Set in 11½/13pt Bembo and 10/12pt Bembo Italic by
Speedset Ltd, Ellesmere Port

Printed and bound in Great Britain by
Mackays of Chatham PLC, Chatham, Kent

British Library Cataloguing in Publication Data
is available on request from the British Library

ISBN 0 09 174668 X

Contents

Acknowledgements

THIS BOOK would not have become a reality without the practical help, advice, friendship and encouragement given so freely by so many trout anglers. In particular I would like to thank: Eric Windley for the vital impetus to start trout fishing, the late Eric Horsfall-Turner for his guidance into tournament casting, Ernest Campbell Black who encouraged me to teach fly-casting, and Geoffrey Serth who gave me the confidence to write.

Tournament casting led me into an advanced world of tackle technology and I would like to extend special thanks to Don Neish, Simon Chilcott and Terry Carroll for rod-making materials, and Terry Collingbourne for state-of-the-art lines.

Without the chance to fish frequently I would not have been able to express my views on fishing based on in-depth experience and careful testing. In this connection I am greatly indebted to: Richard Connell at Ardleigh Reservoir, Bob Buxton late of Cooks Farm, Brian Joslin together with Derek, Fred, Michael, Paul and Tony at Hanningfield Reservoir, Chris Poupard at Aveley Lake and David Weston at Chigborough Fisheries. Their permissions for many photography sessions have also been much appreciated.

I am particularly grateful to Richard Shail for allowing the use of his trout lake to take the jacket photographs and to his son James who appears on the back of the jacket.

Photography has been a crucial element of this project and, in this connection, I am very lucky to have been helped by Peter Gathercole, Mick Toomer and especially Tom Charlton. The outstanding contribution made by my fishing partner and photographer extraordinaire Ken Lynch demands special mention. He was responsible for the jacket pictures and the overhead and roll-casting sequences. To describe these as challenging is an understatement!

Finally my sincere thanks go to my editor Marion Paull for her patience and help. She has made the production of this book a most pleasurable experience which, I hope, is conveyed to my readers in the finished work.

Introduction

I STARTED stillwater fly-fishing 28 years ago with the then-fashionable 9 ft 6 in soft-actioned split-cane rod, a No. 3 double-taper silk line, and the benefit of a ten-minute coaching session from a casting instructor at The Game Fair. Two years of sheer frustration followed. In spite of my reading books on casting, my progress was slow because the texts, as I later realised, lacked the vital detail that could have helped me. Experts, I found, left gaps in the information chain, assuming the reader had knowledge which he hadn't. My main difficulties were with rod-hand movement and line-release time. All the books compared rod movement to the hours on a clock face, but I was never able to 'tell the time'. As for the critical timing of line release, I just hadn't a clue, because my mind was so busy thinking about rod movement.

At last, with regular practice, I developed a reasonable technique, but 'distance' always eluded me. But once I was casting reasonably well, I began to suspect that I was using the wrong rod and line. It was at about this time that the first American tubular glass-fibre rods and plastic-covered fly-lines became available. Not surprisingly, the early rods were no improvement on cane, since the makers were trying to copy the 'action' of traditional cane rods. Then, as an experiment, I tried a few casts with a rod I had made up from the middle and top joints of a light 13-foot glass-fibre salmon rod. The improvement was dramatic. I was able to achieve 'distance' for the first time – and with less physical effort than I had been using previously.

Once properly developed, plastic-covered fly-lines were, in most respects, better than silk. The smooth plastic slid easily through the rod rings, and the floating and variable sink rates permitted great versatility in fly presentation with minimal line maintenance. However, a silk line – for anyone who has one – still casts really

1

well in very still or windy conditions due to its comparatively small diameter and freedom from stretch.

With the benefit of hindsight, I am pleased that I learned my basic casting technique with a double-taper line, unfortunately regarded by many anglers as old-fashioned. But it is vital to be able to perform long, unhurried rod strokes which are the basis of effortless double-taper casting and distance-casting with other lines. Recent teaching experience has revealed that anyone learning with 'high-speed', short weight-forward or shooting-head lines finds great difficulty in slowing down later on.

It was when I joined the British Casting Association and took part in its fly-casting tournaments that I learned to cast really well and to appreciate the full benefits of adapting modern materials. I progressively developed powerful glass-fibre rods and special lines to the stage where winning trophies became a reality, and these developments produced great improvements in my casting performance when scaled down for fishing purposes.

I reluctantly gave up competition casting in 1968 and used my now restricted leisure time to visit the Bristol waters, Chew and Blagdon. With many miles of natural bank to roam, and relatively little angling pressure, I found conditions could be idyllic. But while trout stocks were good, I soon came to appreciate that a better casting technique and better tackle would dramatically improve my catches. Not only would I cover more water, and therefore more trout, but I would also be able to fish for longer periods with a significant reduction in the energy I expended on casting. I would also be able to use light lines for delicate and accurate fly presentation to trout rising at long range and, with heavier equipment, achieve good distances into a strong wind. This is, indeed, what happened.

So many stillwater trout fisheries have been developed since then that, certainly in England, most anglers will find a number within reasonable travelling distance. This is ideal for busy people such as myself, because I can often spare only two hours in late evening, which, in summer, is the best time for fishing anyway. If you would like to have a fishing holiday in the UK, then you really can't do better than contact a fishing hotel. Many are well known and some can be regarded as part of angling history. My own selection starts in Devon and finishes near John o'Groats, and apart from trout fishing, they offer opportunities to fish for salmon and sea-trout as well. Many stillwater trout fishermen seem not to appreciate that their tackle is more than adequate to deal with summer and autumn salmon fishing. In fact, it is often more effective than traditional double-handed rods and heavy lines.

I have had marvellous fun over the years, made many friends, and experienced generosity which will be hard to repay. Trout fishing, because of the relatively small amount of tackle involved, encourages mobility, and therefore more contact with other anglers. This, in turn, promotes friendship and the spread of information which some new trout anglers find surprising. Goodwill is such that on many occasions I have seen an angler move from a productive place or hand over a successful fly from his leader to allow someone less fortunate to catch a trout. Fishing clubs also encourage social intercourse between anglers. Most significant stillwaters have one, and out-of-season social events, talks and demonstrations are often arranged at minimal cost.

A dramatic improvement in rod-making materials has occurred since the late '60s, particularly following the introduction of carbon-fibre. Unfortunately, but with a few exceptions, rod specifications have not improved at the same rate. Rod-makers would help the uninformed angler a great deal if they gave better descriptions of their products, stating not only the recommended AFTM line number, but the rod-action and the normal casting range at which it should be used. Designs for rods with the same line ratings for maximum ranges of 15 yards on rivers and 25 yards on stillwaters should be significantly different. It must be re-membered, too, that fly-fishermen in general do not cast as well as they should!

I started teaching fly-casting professionally nine years ago, and I have had the pleasure of showing many anglers the benefits of good casting. Indeed, I often gain as much satisfaction from their excited telephone calls, following first successes, as from my own fishing. However, their many questions long ago made it clear that published information on fly-casting is inadequate. So what follows is really a collection of answers to problems with which I have had to deal while teaching casting and fishing to anglers at all levels of ability. Some of the unusual methods I suggest may cause raised eyebrows in some quarters, but I can assure you that they work well and have been checked carefully.

My interest in competition casting was rekindled in 1981 following a debate with an old friend on distance-casting theory. I decided to try again, but without appreciating how far tournament casting technology had moved forward. To compete on equal terms, I had to develop new carbon-fibre rods and kevlar-cored lines, and my casting technique had to be refined. All of this was most interesting, but, of course, luck comes into all sporting activities and, in my case, it came in 1983 when I raised the British Trout Distance Record from 65 yards to more than 71 yards. From a fishing point of view, this distance may not be important, but in teaching terms it is vital. Ordinary casting, by comparison, seems to be performed in slow-motion, and it is therefore easy for me to diagnose the casting problems of those anglers attending my clinics.

I then had a busy and absorbing period of 18 months as secretary of the British Casting Association, which gave me a welcome opportunity to make new friends at home and overseas. During this time I came to think that tournament casting had moved too far away from practical fishing, both in level of performance and the power of the equipment used, and I was prompted to organise a Fisherman's Trout Distance Competition as a foundation on which to build.

When teaching I regularly encounter unsuitable and badly matched equipment. Most beginners arrive with a rod that looks nice but has an action which is too soft for stillwater fly-casting. The first need, therefore, is to select a line that will best suit the rod in question. A similar situation arises with experienced anglers who have not found an effective rod, with the result that their casting technique is usually badly flawed. It is not until they start to use my own rod, which is used for teaching and for much of my own trout fishing, that they realise how much improvement is possible. My rod was built from an American carbon-fibre blank which had to be extensively modified to meet my needs, and I have had to refuse requests for duplicates. However, I determined to rectify the situation, and after much development work with a British manufacturer, I did produce a similar rod. Named 'The Grand Prix', it was built to a high-quality specification, was 9 feet long and rated AFTM #8. This type of rod not only eliminates a lot of guesswork for an angler buying for the first time, but provides a reference against which rods for more specialised purposes may be measured. In my case, this involves a whole series of rods, all carefully related to each other in terms of casting power. Most fly-fishermen eventually find the need for two or three rods to meet differing conditions, so the choice can be made on a sound basis.

I have been able to deal effectively with a wide variety of fishing situations on many stillwaters throughout England and Scotland, and with my rod range, I feel well equipped to fish comfortably in stillwaters from one to 1,000 acres, and with depths of up to 50 feet or more. My experience has convinced me that rods and lines should be chosen to match the temperament of the individual angler and the waters he fishes. But I know of no relatively comprehensive guide to enable the inexperienced angler to select fishing that will give him the most enjoyment, considering his personal circumstances and aspirations; or, indeed, to guide the experienced angler who is considering specialisation in a particular branch of fly-fishing.

None of us will ever live long enough to learn all there is to know about fishing techniques appropriate to individual fisheries and different times of the season; and no book would ever be large enough to include all the information available. But armed with the relatively small amount of basic information I am able to give them, many anglers have quickly become experts on the waters they fish. Their expertise undoubtedly develops from a clear understanding of the feeding habits of the trout and what artificial flies the fish will take if they are presented properly. Knowledge produces confidence, and this does much to ensure that the fly in use is attractive to the trout.

Many anglers seem reluctant to take up fly-tying, thinking that the delicacy of the work is beyond them. This makes me sad, because nearly everyone can produce adequate results provided he is shown the correct techniques. Please be encouraged to persist with this worthwhile and rewarding activity. I shall never forget the increased pleasure and interest I gained from fishing following the capture of my first trout on a fly tied in my own vice.

My philosophy has always been that anything learned about sport should be passed on for the benefit of everyone participating. This book is my own written contribution, and I hope it will be of interest to many others. In practical terms I shall continue to teach and to give casting demonstrations. If anyone would like help in these areas, or advice about rods, do not hesitate to write to me, but do, please, send an SAE for my reply!

Michael Marshall
Eskdale, 2 Janmead, Hutton,
Brentwood, Essex CM13 2PU

Stillwater Trout Fishing is Good for You

WHEN ACQUAINTANCES learn that I go trout fishing, they often say something to the effect of, 'God, how have you got the patience to sit there?' This always re-confirms what I have known for years: that people in general know little about fishing of any kind. Sit? Nothing could be further from the truth. Trout fishing is hardly a sedentary pastime, and my rather pained explanations cause considerable surprise!

Trout fishing is a highly active pursuit, quite technical and elegant when practised properly. What more could a modern person want from his or her sport, particularly given the end-product? Have no doubt about it: trout in the freezer lead to an increased circle of friends!

We all need exercise, and trout fishing can be as energetic as you like to make it. In this regard it is excellent, since you do not have to give it up, as you do so many things, as Father Time marches on. For the active person a mile walk in thigh-waders along a reservoir bank, and carrying a bag and rod, is good exercise – particularly the return journey if the catch has been good! On the other hand, smaller waters give plenty of opportunity for the less active to 'take it easy' – but still to take and enjoy exercise.

Fly-casting, done properly, is achieved through flowing muscular co-ordination and requires total concentration, and it alone gives a deep sense of achievement to the accomplished performer. Fishing from the bank and trying to catch trout feeding 35 yards out gives enough exercise to satisfy even the most athletic person, while the short, gentle casting needed when fishing from a boat offers a less strenuous alternative. In either case, the mind is fully occupied and unable to dwell on other problems.

Of all the aspects of trout fishing, casting is the least understood by fishermen, yet even by itself it can give additional interest, and bring extra social contacts, particularly during winter. As a casting instructor, I have first-hand confirmation of this regularly from members of my small groups.

Most large fisheries offer rowing boats for hire, which gives another dimension to fishing. A day out in a boat can be good fun and activate generally unused muscles, particularly if you have to raise and lower an anchor, or pull in a drogue, as well as row. Alternatively, for those preferring a less strenuous day, motor-boats are available on some water-supply reservoirs. These are ideal for fishing in traditional loch-style, drifting broadside to the wind, so again a drogue has to be pulled aboard from time to time. All this physical activity is spread over an extended period while you concentrate on fishing, so it is hardly noticed. But at the end of the day you are left with that pleasantly tired feeling that only sports people can appreciate.

Trout fishers usually generate a relaxed atmosphere often not present in other sports. Golf and tennis thrive on competition, but this is seldom present at the waterside except in the most light-hearted way between friends. Perhaps this is due in part to the setting of fixed limits to the number of fish to be taken by an individual. When the fishing is good, no one seems to be in a hurry, and it is good to see how many newcomers are helped by experienced anglers with advice and successful flies. Even the accomplished fisherman can expect helpful tips when he visits an unfamiliar water, particularly in regard to where fish have been caught recently.

Meeting friends in the clubhouse or the local pub at lunchtime is another relaxation to be enjoyed, but do remember that alcohol has as bad an effect on casting as it does on driving! But such meetings can be absolute goldmines of information, with the bonus of some interesting stories thrown in! I don't usually tell fishing stories, but facts are stranger than fiction, so it does no harm to relate one incident.

I was demonstrating casting at a lake in Berkshire and had attached my usual tuft of red wool, instead of a fly, to my leader. Having cast, I turned to the audience to discuss a point and, while retrieving at the same time, had my wool taken by a large rainbow trout. It jumped twice and made a long run before we parted company, which, of course, caused much amusement! However, it was not the end of the matter. My second rod had been left resting on a small clump of reeds with line, leader and wool tuft in the water. Almost at once the second reel screamed and the rod was nearly pulled into the water before I seized it. After two or three minutes a one and a half pound rainbow was in the net with the wool entangled in its teeth. The disbelief felt by those watching can perhaps be imagined. The unfortunate fish was returned unharmed, but the episode showed that trout fishing is not without interest and incident.

As you become more successful at fly-fishing, you will find more than a passing interest developing in weather patterns, insect-life, birds and trees. These are all important factors in judging fish behaviour and adapting tactics to suit the day. It is the development of a harmony with natural things that separates the successful fisherman from his less effective friends – and it all helps to relieve the stress of modern life. It's not surprising that so many doctors go fishing. They know what's good for them.

A newcomer to trout fishing may have quite a shock when he starts to enquire about fishing possibilities and he finds how many trout lakes he has to choose from. Hundreds of trout fisheries have been created over the last decade, and no one is likely to be too far from one or two of them. Because they are numerous, a day's fishing can be had at reasonable cost compared to that of other activities. Pre-booking is sometimes necessary, but often it's a case of turning up and buying a day-ticket. A major 'plus' is that everything that is needed can simply be taken off the pegs in the garage or wherever with no need to think of buying bait. It all leads to a much more relaxed approach to the water than is possible elsewhere. Trout fishing can also extend the season of the previously confirmed coarse fisherman to a whole year of opportunity. Many have been quick to appreciate the benefits after what has proved an easy transition following tuition from a competent instructor.

Winter is not necessarily a time of inaction. Some fisheries remain open all year, but if winter trout fishing does not appeal, then learning to tie flies will add a new sparkle to next year's trout fishing when you start catching fish on home-tied patterns. Again, the social side of fishing comes to the fore through the many fly-tying courses held throughout the country and advertised regularly in the angling press.

Trout fishing has many interesting facets which bring interest, friends and an active sport that will last a lifetime. A friend often tells me that it is fishing that has kept him sane through all the ups and downs of life, and he enjoys the sport more with each passing year. Yes, it really is good for you, but not until you've learned to cast a fly-line. . . .

Casting Philosophy

AN EXPERIENCED ANGLER, obviously conscious of his limited casting ability, asked me at a demonstration: 'Why should I bother to learn good casting technique? I catch fish now.' This seems to express a commonly held view, but it is one which limits the pleasure fly-fishing should give to those who hold it. Consider the advantages that await a really competent caster. He will be able to:

- Reach and catch trout feeding far out in deep water, particularly early in the year;
- Cast effectively even though backed by a steeply sloping bank or dam wall;
- Cast effectively in strong winds, so prevalent on large waters;
- Fish for long periods without fatigue;
- Cast to rising fish with speed and precision;
- Master side winds which blow the line at him;
- Be a welcome boat-fishing companion;
- Cast lighter, less conspicuous lines good distances;
- Lose fewer flies than others on the bank behind;
- Experience minimum frustration from tangled leaders and wind-knots;
- Give his total concentration to catching fish.

Anyway, that is my sales message, and it is one which I believe makes good sense.

Successful casting depends upon a properly performed sequence of relatively simple muscular movements made at fairly high speed. They are within the scope of almost anyone, whether teenager or retired, provided allowance is made for human variations. People come in all shapes and sizes and vary greatly in muscular co-ordination, so it is vital to reduce casting into steps that are easy to understand and put into action. Nevertheless, great variations must be expected in the times that different people take to succeed. If you feel you are slow, take heart. I was, too! All that is needed is the willingness to practise persistently the methods which I am going to describe.

Fly-casting Theory

I BELIEVE THAT casting flies to catch trout is the most elegant way of fishing and gives the greatest pleasure one can obtain from the sport. For pure excitement, it used to be thought necessary to go salmon fishing, but with salmon-sized trout in many stillwaters, the effort and expense is no longer called for.

Presenting a fly to a trout in the most effective way may be the result of many experiments and much practice, but the underlying and inescapable fact is that the fly-line is the weight which is used to propel the fly to the fish. The line is a string-like weight, and it is perhaps appropriate to think of fly-casting as the art and science of flexible-weight propulsion! It is a pity to sound so technical, but this fundamental point must be made strongly, as so few trout anglers seem to grasp its importance. However, it is easy to forgive this oversight when one considers that an extended fly-line is designed to be as inconspicuous as possible. Coarse and sea anglers have a wide range of immediately recognisable weights for specific purposes. The trout angler must think of his line in similar terms, remembering that the weight is most readily apparent when a coiled line is held in the hand after being unpacked.

Stillwater fly-fishing generally demands the use of two methods of casting, the **overhead cast** and the **roll cast**. The former is used for casting the fly to the fish, the latter for removing a short line from the water before casting again. Each system uses the weight of the line to propel the fly, but in different ways, and it is vital to have a clear idea of what happens during casting. Each system works well, and it is a joy to see an accomplished caster making light work of what may at first sight appear difficult.

THE OVERHEAD CAST

IN THE OVERHEAD CAST, as its name implies, the line remains above head level while it is extended forward and backward. With the fly-rod used as a springy lever, line, leader and fly are lifted backwards clear of the bank or water, allowed to straighten, and then propelled forward on to the water, thus presenting the fly to the fish. The cast is achieved by accelerating line over the rod-tip in extending loops until it is straight behind and in front. Straightness is vital, as the highly flexible line becomes a weight for maximum casting efficiency only when it is under tension from the rod-tip.

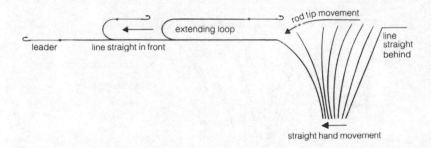

FIGURE 1: *The forward cast*

The simplest form of overhead casting is a sequence of back-and-forward casts with a fixed length of line, which is called **false casting**. The casting action has to be as good backwards as forwards (fly-fishing is virtually the only sporting activity in which you have to perform well backwards!), so it is necessary to be able to turn your head sufficiently to watch the line behind.

The main need is to be able to accelerate the hand holding the rod backwards and forwards in controlled and substantially straight movements of between 20 inches and 30 inches. With a 9-foot rod, and due to arm and slight wrist movement, this will produce a rod-tip movement from back to front of between 75 inches and 110 inches. In calm conditions the same amount of energy should be put into both back and forward casts.

When a cast is performed correctly, the rod accelerates and

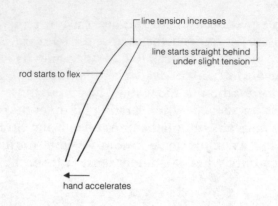

line tension increases

line starts straight behind under slight tension

rod starts to flex

hand accelerates

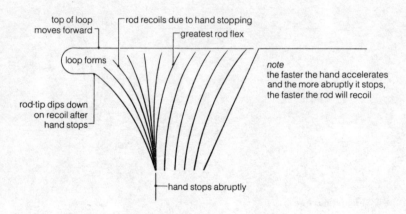

top of loop moves forward

rod recoils due to hand stopping

greatest rod flex

loop forms

note
the faster the hand accelerates and the more abruptly it stops, the faster the rod will recoil

rod-tip dips down on recoil after hand stops

hand stops abruptly

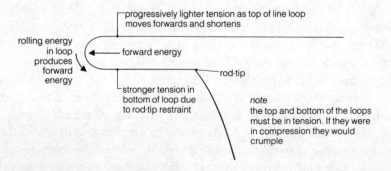

progressively lighter tension as top of line loop moves forwards and shortens

rolling energy in loop produces forward energy

forward energy

rod-tip

stronger tension in bottom of loop due to rod-tip restraint

note
the top and bottom of the loops must be in tension. If they were in compression they would crumple

FIGURE 2: *The forward cast*

recoils, propelling the line over the rod-tip to form an extending loop of forward-rolling energy which is exhausted when the line is straight again. The diagram will perhaps make the action clearer.

While the top of the loop possesses its own forward momentum from the initial rod-tip acceleration, it is kept in tension by the rolling forces generated in the loop. This tension is light and is the difference between the increased rolling force and the initial forward momentum of the top of the line loop. Stronger tension exists in the bottom of the loop due to the line being restrained by the rod-tip until it is fully extended. At this moment the line will fall, under the force of gravity, unless another cast is made in the opposite direction.

The main purpose of casting is to increase the line length between angler and fly to a fish-catching distance, and this is achieved by using the tension produced in the bottom of the loop. The forward cast is accelerated faster than in false casting, allowing a controlled increase in the length of the bottom of the loop to be made while the loop is moving forward. Provided the timing and control of this increase is correct, sufficient tension will be produced in the bottom of the loop to maintain the line profile throughout the cast.

THE ROLL CAST

THE ROLL CAST is used in stillwater fishing mainly for removing a fly-line from the water ready for the next overhead cast. It also has an application when obstructions lie behind the caster, but this is unusual.

The cast is begun with the line retrieved to 7–8 yards and the rod brought behind the caster to make an angle of 45–50 degrees to the horizontal. With the line moving slowly backwards, the rod-tip is briskly rolled forward. It acts at first against a short length of line weight, but as it rolls further forward, a large backward loop starts to form. The weight of line acting on the rod-tip is small compared to that acting at the start of the overhead cast. However, once the loop above the water is rolling nicely, another form of weight – the apparent weight of the line under or on the water – increases rod-flex. This apparent weight and, therefore, tension in the bottom of the loop is caused by the frictional resistance of the line against the water. A satisfactory roll cast cannot be made without this friction, as anyone who has tried it on, say, grass will verify!

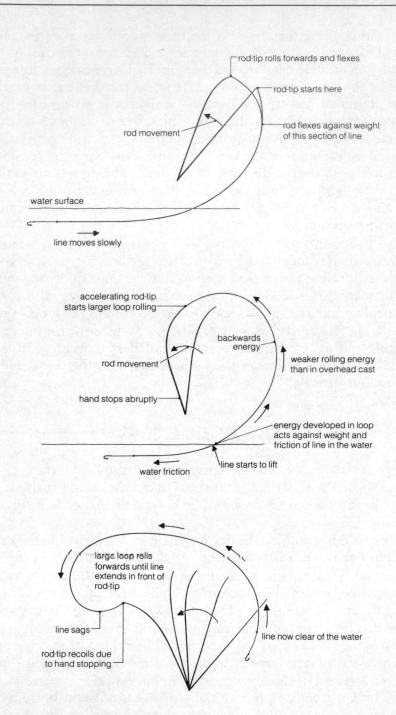

rod-tip rolls forwards and flexes

rod-tip starts here

rod flexes against weight of this section of line

rod movement

water surface

line moves slowly

accelerating rod-tip starts larger loop rolling

backwards energy

weaker rolling energy than in overhead cast

rod movement

hand stops abruptly

energy developed in loop acts against weight and friction of line in the water

water friction

line starts to lift

large loop rolls forwards until line extends in front of rod-tip

line sags

rod-tip recoils due to hand stopping

line now clear of the water

FIGURE 3: *The roll cast*

As the rod continues to roll and recoil forwards, a large but effective loop forms in front of the rod-tip, which then behaves as in the overhead cast. By this time the whole line is drawn backwards and upwards from the water, and, under the forward loop action, is eventually rolled in front of the rod-tip. In this position, the relatively short line will be sagging downwards, but it will be sufficiently straight to provide the basic weight for an overhead back-cast.

Fly-casting Training

I HAVE ALWAYS BEEN fascinated by the various actions and stances adopted by beginners when they use a rod for the first time. Despite a thorough briefing, their preoccupation with force seems to cause a total loss of co-ordination. In view of this perpetual problem, I have developed a system of training those parts of the body involved to perform in the correct manner without the distracting influence of a rod, its main advantage being that it can be practised at home at any time.

The secret of casting well is to repeat the appropriate movements precisely, individually and collectively, without thinking about them. This is more difficult than might be thought, even for an experienced angler, so please give the following exercises an extended trial. The descriptions and diagrams are drawn for right-handed casters. Left-handers will have mentally to alter them to suit.

HAND GRIP

WE ALL USE the expression 'get a grip', and its application is never more important than in fly-casting. The four fingers of the casting hand should be around the largest, central part of the rod handle, with the thumb up the back of the rod and directly opposite the reel and rod rings. A ¼-inch movement of the thumb caused by turning the wrist joint from front to back or side to side produces a movement of 4½ inches at the tip of a 9-foot rod, so a movement of this magnitude will have a significant bearing on what the line does when it is in motion.

The grip on the rod handle should be firm enough to prevent the rod moving within the fingers, but not really tight. Too hard a grip

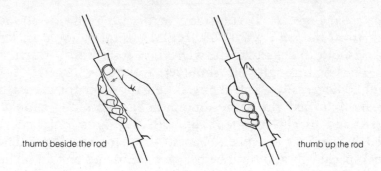

thumb beside the rod   thumb up the rod

FIGURE 4: *Hand grips*

causes the forearm and upper arm muscles to tighten up, which, in turn, spoils the arm action, which should be smooth and flowing.

To illustrate the importance of the 'thumb-up-the-rod' grip, try this experiment:

- Hold your hand out in front, in line with your shoulder and at ear height.
- Form a grip around an imaginary rod handle with the thumb vertical.
- Using the wrist joint only, angle the thumb tip forward by ¼ inch and then move it back to the vertical. Now move it backwards for ¼ inch and then back to the vertical. Repeat this for side-to-side movements.
- Having got the hang of the movements, repeat them with your eyes shut.
- Now try to repeat the same angular movements with the 'thumb-beside-the-rod' grip.

You will find precise control easy with the 'thumb up', but uncertain with the 'thumb beside'. Good wrist control is essential in casting and must be performed instinctively because you will be watching the line.

—— HAND AND ARM MOVEMENTS ——

IF YOU WISH the line to go backwards and forwards straight and level, it is logical to train your hand movements to work likewise. To do this, select a straight garden cane of, say, 4 ft 6 in and hang it horizontally with string on a convenient wall at the same height as the top of your ear. Now take up the normal casting position (*see diagram, page 21*). If you stand with your right ear about 18 inches from the wall, your forearm and thumb should make an angle of about 15 degrees to the wall when your thumb touches the cane. The line through your shoulders should be turned between 15 and 20 degrees towards the wall (left shoulder forwards), and your head turned the same amount. The left foot should be forward and parallel to the wall, with the right foot back and turned 20 degrees to the wall. Front-to-back toe-spacing and heel-to-heel spacing should both be between 12 inches and 14 inches.

Keeping your thumb vertical, move it backwards along the cane until it is uncomfortable to take it any further, which should be 6–7 inches behind your ear. Now, move your thumb forwards until your arm is nearly straight, which should place it 18–20 inches in front of your ear. Don't turn your head or twist your shoulders. Everyone has different proportions, so adjust your feet slightly until you have the best balance and most comfortable arm movement while maintaining the 15-degree forearm and thumb angle to the cane. Repeat the arm movement gently until you can do it with your eyes shut.

A useful tip is to say 'push' as your hand moves forwards and 'pull' as it moves backwards. If you do this routinely, you will start saying it to yourself when you are actually casting, which will be a great help in creating the correct rhythm. Despite the fact that the cane is horizontal and straight, you should become conscious of some unexpected sensations. When moving your hand forwards, you will feel that it is going up and away from you; when moving it backwards, your feeling will be that your hand is being pushed down and towards you. It is important to become accustomed to these movements and feelings as to do otherwise will cause problems. It is also important to notice that your right elbow rises slightly as your hand goes forwards.

One of the secrets of effortless casting is to use the 6-7 inches of shoulder movement that can be gained by rocking backwards and forwards from the ankles. Imagine an upside-down pendulum, and practise the movement by using a modified 'cane system'. Start by rocking slightly forwards, so that your body-weight is transferred to the balls of the feet as the arm moves progressively to the fully-forward position, with the thumb touching the cane. Now move the thumb backwards as you rock slightly backwards, transferring your body-weight to your heels. If you mark the new fully-forward and fully-backward thumb positions, you should find that you have achieved an increase of at least 20 per cent

FIGURE 6: *Cane and string*

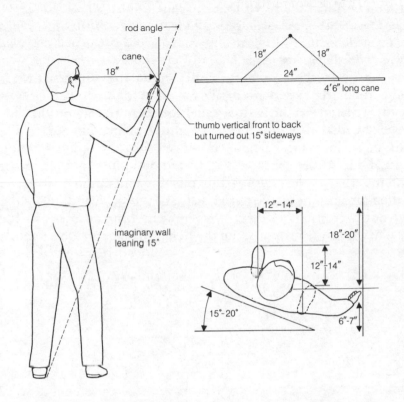

rod angle

cane

18"

18"

18"

24"

4'6" long cane

thumb vertical front to back
but turned out 15° sideways

imaginary wall
leaning 15°

12"–14"

18"–20"

12"–14"

15°–20°

6"–7"

FIGURE 5: *Normal casting position*

compared with your stationary body position. This gain is extremely useful in casting a long line, the increased rod–travel being used to accelerate the line over a greater distance. Repetition of the procedure until you can move the thumb along the cane without loss of balance is vital to improving your technique.

Now tilt the front of the cane downwards about 6 inches so that it makes an angle to the floor and, maintaining your feet, body and hand positions as before, run the thumb along it again. This should be done backwards and forwards as before, but without rocking the body at first (*see diagram, page 22*). Repeat the procedure with the front of the cane tilted upwards 6 inches. If you were fishing, this would cause the fly to be cast on to the bank behind and perhaps be lost – a very common problem. However, if you remember the cause from the start, you will be able to avoid the consequences in the long term. Practise until you can 'feel' the muscular sensations, repeat all the movements with your eyes shut, and perform them without the cane.

The importance of these movements cannot be over-emphasised. When you can perform them instinctively, you will find that many casting problems will simply disappear.

My practical teaching experience has shown me that most casters – and particularly experienced casters – tend to move their elbows and upper arms very little. It is usual for them to rely on the old-fashioned radial forearm and wrist movements, likened to the hands of a clock face. These, however, greatly reduce casting potential due to the creation of a wide line loop. Another major problem is that anglers false cast by pushing and pulling correctly, but then, during the last forward cast, start to push and then chop downwards from the elbow joint, which completely spoils the cast. They do this, I suppose, in the belief that a large downwards

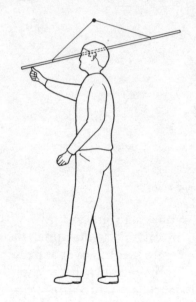

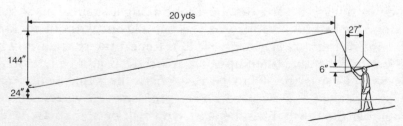

FIGURE 7: *Cane tilted down at front*

motion is needed to place the line on the water. It is not. All that is needed is to follow the cane in its downward-tilted position to generate the right movement. The diagram shows that it is necessary to tilt the cane down only 6 inches to straighten a line 2 ft above the water at approximately 20 yards.

If you really wish to improve your casting, you must appreciate that time and effort are needed to eradicate a bad habit of long standing. It is easy to say 'I can do it on the day' and leave it at that when the real need is for regular training for reluctant muscles.

HEAD MOVEMENT

THE BACK-CAST, as I have mentioned, also needs to be done well, so it pays to be able to look round to see what is going on behind. Unfortunately, most necks are not as flexible as they might be, so a little practice is needed.

Stand with both shoulders about 2 inches from a wall with your head facing straight ahead. Now turn your head gently to the right, looking behind out of the corner of your right eye. Then return to the straight-ahead position. Keep practising the movement and speed it up, but do not strain at it at any time – and, yes, it might be as well to do it in private!

The object of this exercise is to enable you to see the line behind you without turning your shoulders, and, plainly, your shoulders will not turn if they touch the wall. Rotational movement of the shoulders spoils the straight forward-and-backward alignment we try so hard to achieve in a good cast.

CASTING ACTION

THE DYNAMIC hand-and-arm movement needed in casting is difficult to describe. It is easy to demonstrate in practical teaching because I stand behind the caster and actually cast with him, clasping my hand over his. However, I discovered a way of simulating casting action quite by accident while I was cleaning a paint-brush. This is how it works. . . .

Select a clean 2½–3-inch paint-brush and pour some water in a suitable container. Now stand in any open area with 15–20 ft clear space in front, making sure that any breeze is coming from left to right and that no damage will be done by a little spray. Take up the normal casting position (*see diagram, page 21*), remembering the straight-along-the-cane movement with your forearm turned outwards 15 degrees. Dip the brush in the water and take it to the rearmost casting position. The thumb should be up, behind the brush handle and tilted back about half an inch behind the vertical.

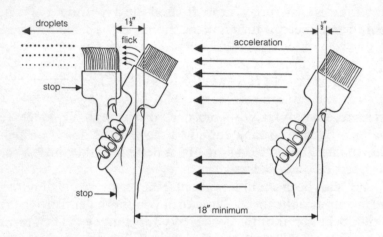

FIGURE 8: *Paint-brush and water 'casting'*

From this stationary position, push your hand forwards, moving it progressively faster, with the thumb angled back. As you reach the maximum forward position, stop your arm and 'flick' your hand forward with a slight movement of the wrist joint, with the thumb stopping about one inch in front of the vertical. The movement should be smooth, with the arm accelerating from slow to fast and with the very small wrist movement blended in. The more abruptly the arm and hand stop, the crisper the 'flick' will be and the further the water droplets will go. Now dip the brush in the water again and try to shoot the droplets as far forward as possible in a level plane, looking only at the top line of droplets and ignoring the lower spray. The water will go quite a long way if you keep your hand moving horizontally in a straight line and do not 'flick' the thumb too far forward and downward. You should quickly reach 20 feet.

It is not stretching the imagination too far to think of the bristles as a large number of miniature fishing rods, but you must use plenty of arm movement, as you do when training with the cane. It is possible to 'cheat' by using a short hand travel, but this does not help in the long term. In casting it is vital to be able to accelerate the rod with AT LEAST 18 inches of hand movement, so it is necessary to do the same with the brush to achieve the correct simulation.

Imagine the cane tilted up at the front. 'Flick' the water forward and high, then forward and low. Once you have mastered this, you will have a full appreciation of the arm and hand movements needed for successful forward casting.

Now we come to the difficult part! Try reversing the process, and if you don't find it more difficult, you are lucky. Be consoled by the thought that it is worse with a rod and line. Remember, the back-cast is the foundation of a good forward cast and *vice versa*, so keep practising. With persistence and good control you will soon be able to perform nearly as well backwards as forwards, and at different angles, too. When 'casting' backwards, turn your head to watch the droplets and make sure you are using the correct length of hand travel. It is more natural to use a short backward movement, but the temptation must be resisted.

Make sure the water droplets go out along a straight line front and back, as if you were throwing along a wall leaning 15 degrees. If they don't go straight, either your hand is not 'moving along the cane' or your shoulders are twisting. Should the water droplets not be travelling more than 12–15 feet, you are not accelerating the forearm, or 'flicking', fast enough. In boxing terms, the end of the forearm movement should be such that you would give someone a sharp 'dig' rather than trying to knock him over with a heavy blow.

The aim is to cause the rod-tip to recoil, thus driving the line forward. The action and effect might be compared to accelerating a car hard and then braking equally hard: but for the seat-belt, you would be catapulted forward. The method is a good one for achieving the fast line speed that many beginners find so elusive. As with most things, once a positive start has been made, progress is then continuous.

At this point a cautionary tale about pets is in order if normal friendly relations are to be maintained. I was practising with the brush one day when, unnoticed, our very curious and affectionate Blue Point cat walked across the lawn behind me, just as I was 'letting go' with a particularly well executed low back-cast. Unfortunately, this transformed his rather aristocratic long-haired appearance into that of a low grade mop!

25

CONCLUSION

I HOPE THAT having practised the basic elements of casting I have described, you now have a clear picture of what you need to do and how to do it – and all without having touched a fly-rod or line!

If you are an experienced angler, wishing to improve, I strongly recommend that you do not 'skip' any of the steps. A small and elementary discrepancy often gives rise to a frustrating flaw in performance – the most common being a downward chop with the hand and forearm, particularly on the final forward cast.

No training methods are proposed, or indeed are necessary, for roll casting. Not only is the cast usually made with a short line, but arm movement is small. Once you have learned to make a good overhead cast, you will quickly master the roll cast if you follow the instructions given on page 90.

Remember, all the training methods I have outlined may be practised without need to buy any tackle. Now, however, we must think about what is needed.

Basic Tackle

You'll not often find me advising the spending of large sums of money on fishing, but with rods, it pays to buy the best. The best may not necessarily be the most expensive, but often it does work out that way.

Modern rods are extremely light and are made from glass-, carbon-, boron- or kevlar-fibre materials. Glass-fibre rods are usually cheaper than carbon, and carbon rods are cheaper than the others. I use carbon rods, but should your funds extend only to glass, then don't worry. Glass will do nicely to start with.

Carbon rods offer three main advantages:

- They have a faster, crisper action than glass and cast further as a result.
- Being lighter, they are less tiring to use, particularly over a whole day.
- Their diameter is slimmer than glass, allowing them to slice through wind better.

All fly-rods are marked with an AFTM number or numbers, which appear with the symbol #. These indicate the weights of line the rod is designed to cast, the higher numbers indicating heavier lines. For stillwater fly-fishing the usual numbers are #6/7 for delicate fishing, #7/8 for the bulk of general fishing, and #8/9 for long-range and deep-down fishing. The reason for two numbers is straightforward. A rod will handle an optimum weight of line outside the rod-tip and this weight can be achieved with, say, a shorter #8 or a longer #7 line. However, it is vital to know which line weight produces the best results, and this is not always explained. This problem has been compounded by some rods

27

displaying even more AFTM numbers, which is stretching the optimum performance concept too far!

Because long experience is needed properly to judge the optimum line to be used with a particular rod, a change to a one-number system would eliminate a great deal of confusion. For example, if a rod were rated #8 (for general-purpose fishing), the purchaser would know exactly which lines to buy for normal conditions. Equally, he would appreciate that a longer #7 line could be cast in good conditions, whereas a shorter #9 line could be used to combat rough weather. However, powerful casters should remember that, particularly with double-taper lines, a length (and therefore weight) can be extended beyond which a particular rod cannot cast.

I have never noticed much difference between distances cast by rods, say, of 9 feet and 9 feet 6 inches. The right *rod action* is far more important than length if you are to achieve good performance. You might think that a longer rod will provide a higher back-cast, but good arm action more than compensates, and a longer rod is more tiring to use, particularly over extended periods.

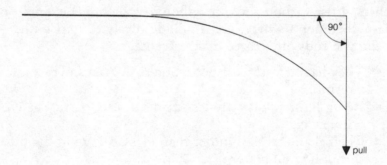

FIGURE 9: *Good rod action*

A good rod action is 'middle-to-tip', and it should be judged by pulling the rod-tip at 90 degrees to the handle with a piece of string knotted to the tip ring or a line threaded through all the rings. The line will be within a few degrees of this position towards the end of the casting stroke, so it makes good sense to test in this way. It is much more important to use a rod having the correct action and stiffness than to have one of unusual appearance or made from exotic and unnecessarily expensive materials. Furthermore, pay no attention to advertisements for rods claiming to have 'explosive power' or something similar. If such power exists, it comes from the caster.

One real problem is in judging whether a rod is stiff enough for stillwater casting. Unfortunately, various rods given the same AFTM numbers exhibit dissimilar characteristics, presumably because their designers have different fishing situations in mind. For instance, a #7 rod made for river fishing at an average range of, say, 12 yards will need to be considerably less stiff than a stillwater rod which is expected to cast nearly twice that distance. It is the line-weight outside the rod-tip that dictates the stiffness needed.

A simple test can be applied to judge the correct stiffness of the 9-foot #8 carbon stillwater rod which I recommend for a beginner. Ask a friend to hold the rod's cork handle, rings uppermost, on a book placed on a table, and align the tip ring with a convenient fixed point. Now gently hang a coiled double-taper #8 line at the tip and measure the vertical deflection. This should be between 11 inches and 13 inches. Less than 11 inches indicates a stiff action unsuitable for beginners; more than 13 inches suggests that the rod is designed for shorter casting on rivers.

FIGURE 10: *Rod stiffness test*

Rod rings should be of the modern oxide-lined type throughout. These allow a line to slide through smoothly, and offer a considerable advantage over wire rings in distance-casting. Also, they enable delicate offers from fish to be felt much better, and their resistance to grooving means that they last longer. The bottom ring will have two legs, and the intermediates a single-leg mounting.

Rod handles should be of a design that prevents your hand slipping along the rod and not be less than ⅞ of an inch in diameter at the centre; otherwise they will be difficult to grip properly (unless you have a smaller-than-average hand). A firm grip allows the rod to be controlled precisely, whereas a tight grip causes the arm muscles to tense up and tire – and that is much more likely to happen with a small-diameter handle. The reel should be as near to the hand as possible, with a short extension behind.

It is often suggested that a reel should balance a rod, but this is not so during casting, when most energy is expended. In an overhead cast the rod is used within about 30 degrees of the vertical, and the weight of the reel, on its very short lever in relation to the wrist fulcrum, has a minute counterbalancing effect on the rod-tip. More important, when the rod-tip is 'flicked' forwards or backwards at the end of the arm acceleration, the weight of the reel must be moved in the opposite direction, to the other side of the wrist fulcrum. Basic mechanics tell us that the closer the weight is to the pivot, the less turning effort the wrist has to make. This is not insignificant in a whole day's fishing. In fishing out a cast, the rod is nearer to the horizontal and it might be argued that the reel should be further away from the hand to balance the rod. However, carbon rods are now so light that their weight is hardly noticed. The short extension behind the reel is useful in restricting angular wrist movement during training and, of course, keeps the reel off the ground when the rod is stood up. It also helps to keep the reel away from clothing when a fish is being played.

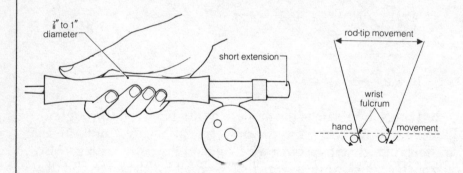

FIGURE 11: *Good handle design*   FIGURE 12: *Reel angular movement*

Reels are no more than holders for storing line and backing, and for letting out or retrieving line while a fish is being played. Having many lines, I go for quantity rather than quality, but I can understand anyone wishing to have at least one expensive reel simply for aesthetic reasons. Lightness of construction is important in a reel in helping to reduce fatigue. A large-diameter reel allows line to be retrieved quickly if it is well filled, and line and backing are less inclined to coil, as they may if they have been tightly wound on a small-diameter spool. (Coiled backing is inclined to tangle!) A wide spool holds a good reserve of backing, which is important when large fish are expected. Good reels also have a smooth, adjustable ratchet check and interchangeable spools with exposed rims to permit finger-drag to be applied. My ideal reel is at least 3⅝ inches in diameter and ²⁹⁄₃₂ of an inch wide inside the spool, with a weight of no more than 4½ ounces. Some recently developed metal and strong plastic reels meet these criteria, though metal reels may bend if dropped, whereas plastic reels tend to bounce.

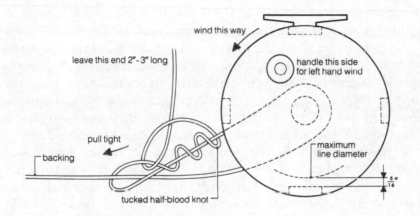

FIGURE 13: *Assembled reel for left-hand wind*

No reel should be over-filled with line. If it is, uneven line winding and the consequent risk of line binding in the reel frame could lose you fish. With the line level across the spool, clearance of ⁵⁄₁₆ of an inch from the reel frame is essential. Filling a reel accurately is easy if the fly-line is wound on the spool first, then the backing on top until the correct level is reached. Backing and line should then be stripped off and laid neatly over a clear area before being rewound, backing first. Under no circumstances should the line be left wound on the small-diameter spool centre for long, because it will become permanently coiled. Knot the end of the backing around the spool centre with a tucked half-blood knot, leaving the spare end 2–3 inches long. Pull the knot tight, slide it down to the spool centre, and tighten it sufficiently to grip the spool and permit winding. The loose end, which should be bound down, is useful for pulling the knot out again if necessary, since it is difficult to cut backing at the spool centre when a change is needed.

The backing should be wound on the spool under moderate tension in fairly coarse spirals across the spool's width. This prevents outer layers cutting-in and being trapped by the inner turns, or, worse, being pulled down between the side of the spool and the backing coils. Should either mishap occur while a fish is being played, the chances are that the leader will break. To achieve satisfactory tension and coarse spirals, I mount the reel on the butt section of a rod and wind in while pinching and guiding the backing with my index finger and thumb, always watching for the inherent twist that some braided backing has which can 'build-up' in front of the pinch as I wind. It is essential to remove this potential source of tangles by stopping from time to time, taking the reel off, and twisting it in the opposite direction.

Anglers argue about the merits of left-hand winding as opposed to right-hand winding. The case for left-hand winding by a right-handed angler is clear. Many stillwater fisheries hold large trout, sometimes as large as the average salmon, and it is wise to anticipate the capture of a big fish and the problems of a long battle. The most important factor in playing a big trout is to hold the rod in your stronger hand. After ten minutes your right arm will really start to suffer, but your left would be far worse! Left-hand winding is not always easy to start with, but it is worth the effort, particularly when you do not have to change the rod to the other hand to wind in just as a hooked trout turns awkward.

Ratchet checks must be set for your chosen direction of winding. They have a stronger click action when rotating in one direction than in the other. Adjust the internal mechanism (which can vary according to make) so that the fish pulls the stronger ratchet and you wind against the weaker one. Some reels incorporate an extra ratchet spring which is a great help if a spring breaks. A reel with a silent drag often enables a particularly active trout to be landed more quickly than it would be on one with a ratchet, because vibrations are not transmitted down the line and leader. I frequently notice the same effect when I play a trout by pulling and releasing line by hand rather than off the reel with a ratchet.

LINE-TRAYS

WHAT DOES ONE DO with the slack line retrieved as a cast is fished out? The longer the cast, the more slack is produced and the greater the problem of 'storing' it tidily until the next cast.

The 'figure-of-eight' method of retrieving results in line being stored in the hand, and a very good method it is (*see page 37*). However, it is not suitable for all types of line, particularly shooting-heads, and it does not allow a fast retrieve. Dropping the line on the bank is a common method of coping with the problem, but it has disadvantages. A line will eventually be damaged by being trodden on and rod rings will suffer from applications of grit!

An item of equipment which overcomes these problems, and those caused by wind tangles and wading, is a line-tray. This is a deep, framed canvas tray which is worn on a belt around the waist and into which the line is placed. Several makes are available and good tackle-shops will have a choice to suit individual budgets and needs. My advice is to buy one. You will not regret it, particularly when conditions are rough or you are wading.

When you are practising casting, which may well be on smooth-cut grass, no harm will be done by letting the line or backing fall to the ground.

LINES

UNLIKE OUR FOREBEARS, who had severely limited options with lines, we are spoiled for choice, with a huge range of plastic-coated, braided-core lines, from high-floaters, through slow-sinkers, to extra-fast sinkers. Added to these are sink-tips, various 'profiles', and a wide selection of colours. Indeed, the choice is mind-boggling. Having said this, the modern fly-line is an absolutely superb long, flexible and precise weight which allows us to present artificial flies to the trout efficiently and delicately.

The lines most used for stillwater fly-fishing are rated AFTM #6, 7, 8 and 9, and their weights are given in the table below. These are average figures and are subject to tolerances in manufacturing.

AFTM number	Total weight of first 30 feet of double-taper line in **grains** (approx.)	Weight of double-taper central belly section in **grains** per foot (approx.)
#6	160	6.0
#7	185	7.0
#8	210	8.0
#9	240	9.0

To convert grains to ounces, multiply by 0.00229. To convert grains to grams, multiply by 0.0648. The table of weights applies to any line, whether floating or sinking.

DOUBLE-TAPER (DT) LINES AND BACKINGS

LINES USED for stillwater fishing have three configurations or 'profiles': double-taper (DT); weight-forward (WF) or forward-taper; and the shooting-taper or shooting-head (ST).

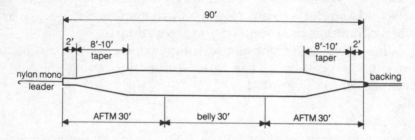

FIGURE 14: *A double-taper line*

The double-taper (DT) line is the same at both ends and can be reversed if one end becomes worn. The taper is vital to the gentle presentation of the fly, because as the taper moves progressively into the line loop, less rolling and forward energy is produced so the end of the line turns over with minimum disturbance. One hears the DT line branded as old-fashioned, but I regard it as the basic line with which to learn to cast, and it is invaluable for certain fishing purposes.

It is important for the newcomer to fly-casting to learn to be able to keep the line in the air by accelerating it backwards and forwards. The DT line is the best one for this. It allows *an ideal casting length to match the angler, and his rod to be pulled from the reel* and gives the advantage that a thickish piece of line can be held in the left hand. This is a real benefit, since most beginners tend to let the line slip or go when it should not. The uniformly thick line passing up through the rod rings and into the line loop gives a feeling of line-flow during casting which is not present with other lines, and the weight of the top 4–5 feet of line in the rod rings causes the rod to flex more than it might otherwise.

The DT is the only line to use if you wish to cast more than, say, 15 yards into a strong wind, which you should be able to do when competent. It will also penetrate 'dead-air' conditions, while straightening the leader really well. The reason for this good performance is that 'heavy line' is always running from the left hand and up through the rod rings, thus causing additional tension in the bottom of the loop. The tension is caused by the weight of the column of line and its associated friction in the rod rings, which, in turn, create more forward energy, thus turning the loop over effectively into wind. For the same reason, it will also cast across a strong side wind with the least possible downwind deflection. Discussion over the years about 'invisible walls' and the like has been due to a lack of understanding about DT line performance.

The lifting of 15–17 yards of floating line off the water without shortening line, so as to be able to cast quickly to rising fish, can be satisfactorily accomplished only with a DT line. Again, this is possible because the uniformly thick line to the rod-tip can be accelerated into a back-cast, then cast straight to the trout. Weight-forward lines have to be retrieved until the thinner backing line is completely within the rod rings, because it does not have sufficient weight to start a line loop rolling from the rod-tip.

The method of casting a DT line is to start with about 6 yards of line and to cast backwards and forwards perhaps 8 feet above the water, shooting another 3–4 yards in the process. This sequence is repeated three or four times until the maximum length you can comfortably manage is reached. The line should not touch the water at any time until the last forward cast is made. Obviously, the more line you can shoot on each forward cast, the fewer intermediate casts will be needed and the less tiring your fishing will be. An accomplished caster can shoot line during the back-cast as well, but this is unusual. In good conditions, with a light breeze from behind, an average caster should be able to cast 20–21 yards with a DT line, including the leader, and a good caster 25–26 yards.

My experience is that a DT line shoots much better through oxide-lined rod rings than through wire rings. The latter always seem to cause the line to grate somewhat as it shoots through, particularly if both rings and line show signs of good, honest wear. This becomes even more evident when the double-haul casting technique is used.

One way of helping the leader to straighten in difficult conditions is to restrict the amount of shoot during the last forward cast. In good conditions you might shoot 5–6 yards during this last cast, having completely released the line from the left hand. However, by restricting line-flow by gradually closing the left hand around the line, you achieve a braking effect, which causes a further increase in the tension in the bottom of the line loop, thus turning the line-end and leader over more vigorously. The DT line is, by reason of its larger belly diameter, the easiest to control with the left hand during fishing. It is also less prone to tangle than other lines.

An outstanding example of the efficiency of the DT line occurred at Hanningfield Reservoir in Essex, one rough May day. The wind was blowing strongly from the south-west across two miles of water, pushing waves half-way up the dam wall. It was also blowing lots of food into one corner, where the trout were feeding greedily. Using my 9-foot #8 rod with a DT #8 medium-sink line, a 6-foot 8 lb breaking-strain leader and a size 12 Black Chenille fly, and with smooth, powerful accelerations, letting the rod do most of the work, I managed to drive 18–19 yards of line into the teeth of the wind in three 'shoots'. The leader did not straighten well, but it was short and little fishing distance was lost. Nor indeed did the fish mind the slight splash of the line, which I'd cast low over the water to avoid it being blown back after straightening. I retrieved with a brisk 'figure-of-eight', to avoid line tangles, and within the hour I had taken a six-fish limit of rainbows totalling 18 pounds 6 ounces after some of the most exciting battles I'd ever had. Landing the fish involved literally drawing them into a long-handled net on the crest of a wave.

It is the triumph over adversity, and a rewarding catch such as this, which make the time and trouble taken to learn good casting technique so worthwhile.

The main advantages of the figure-of-eight retrieve are that all the line is stored in the left hand, where it cannot be influenced by wind or water. In re-casting, the line is released progressively with each 'shoot'. As with casting, the technique has to be learned properly if a tangle-free bunching is to be achieved, but patience will soon bring good results.

Hanningfield was the setting for another more recent example of good DT line performance. The summer had been a non-event as far as evening fishing was concerned, due to continually fluctuating weather conditions. One simply never knew what to expect from hour to hour, and the evening in question was no exception. It was rather cool, with the breeze blowing from the

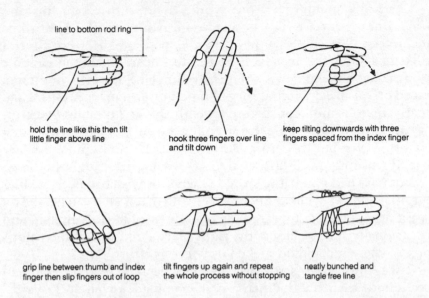

line to bottom rod ring

hold the line like this then tilt little finger above line

hook three fingers over line and tilt down

keep tilting downwards with three fingers spaced from the index finger

grip line between thumb and index finger then slip fingers out of loop

tilt fingers up again and repeat the whole process without stopping

neatly bunched and tangle free line

FIGURE 15: *Figure-of-eight retrieve*

south-east and along the dam wall from my left, and I had decided to use a #8 medium-sinking shooting-head to cover as much water as possible. Having ascertained that virtually nothing had been caught, I adopted 'shock tactics' in the form of a size 10 fluorescent-pink Tadpole, though without much confidence.

After half an hour without an offer, the prospect of an early night became quite attractive. But wait! What breeze there was suddenly died as conditions became overcast and decidedly humid, but pleasantly warmer. The water's surface assumed an oily look, and then a trout rose and started to 'vacuum' a few invisible insects (to me, anyway) from the surface. Going against all fishing theory, I quickly retrieved my line and made a speculative cast to the fish. The fly plopped in just in front of and beyond the fish, and the first draw brought it right in front of its nose as it made a slight hump in the surface film. The fish took gently and a good scrap culminated in my landing a 2¼-pound rainbow.

A few more fish were now showing, but thinking that my ploy wouldn't work twice, I quickly changed to a #8 DT floating line. A tapered leader knotted together from three 3-foot lengths of 15-pound, 10-pound and 7-pound nylon was attached to the line loop and the same pink Tadpole knotted to the point. The whole leader was then degreased with detergent powder and a drop of water.

Every few minutes a trout would swim into range, making bulges in the surface film as it fed on a random path. After three unsuccessful attempts at plotting the path of the next riser, I managed to put the fly in front of a trout's nose. Again the Tadpole was taken on the first draw. The fish jumped 3 feet into the air and raced off on an electrifying run followed by two more jumps. I had many anxious moments before I weighed it at 2 pounds 7 ounces. What sport! Three more trout ended up in my bag before that eventful evening drew to a close, and as far as I could see, my friends, fishing much further along the dam, had caught nothing.

But why had a pink lure scored when those fish had been feeding on small pupae? Well, in my opinion, and that is all it can be, the fly was fairly buoyant, appeared lively because of its flowing tail, and occasionally moved in just the right place – in front of the trout's nose, where it could be sucked in without effort.

It was in this last factor that the DT line and tapered leader had come into their own. When a cast was made, even at 20-yards' range, the central belly caused the loop to drive out, straightening the line and tapered leader. 'Dead-air' did not affect presentation, so I could concentrate on 'chasing' the trout with my fly. Sometimes I made three casts to the same fish as it weaved about, but the line could be taken straight into a back-cast and then re-cast with appropriate adjustments to length and direction. Occasionally I lined a trout, which was the signal for a mighty swirl as the fish dived in fright.

Conditions are at their most demanding when no pattern in fish-movement is apparent, and it is largely a waste of time to 'fish the water' because the odds are too much against the fish seeing the fly. So it was much better, on the evening in question, to cast to a few predictable risers rather than many erratic ones, even if the fly was quite unusual. Given the same accuracy of casting, I am sure that any good-sized pupa imitation would have been taken well, but I had no time for experiment. I was lucky to have a first positive response to give me a much-needed clue! In retrospect, I might have done even better had I fished with a DT #7 line during the calm, but I had not bothered to take one with me in the initially breezy conditions.

Side drift – DT floating line

Good though the DT line usually is, it also has some disadvantages. One is that when a floating line is retrieved slowly across a fairly strong wind-driven current, the pressure on the comparatively thick line, particularly near the rod-tip, causes the fly to drag. On large waters this drag may continue for a long time after the wind has dropped, because once a large volume of water starts to circulate, it takes some time to stop.

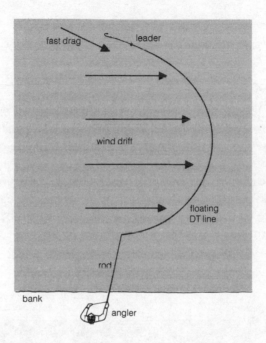

FIGURE 16: *Side drift, DT line*

Drag takes place in a curved path across the current, giving an unnatural speed to a small fly. Unfortunately, it is not easy to gain control in this situation, since efforts to rectify the curve usually result in an unacceptable stop-start movement being imparted to the fly.

Sinking characteristic – DT line

A sinking DT line can cause problems when it is fished over a gently sloping bottom typical of reservoir margins. The heaviest part of the line is closest to the rod and over the shallowest water which causes the line to lie on the bottom or be close to it, with the result that the fly is drawn into any weed or debris.

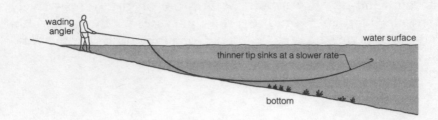

FIGURE 17: *Sinking characteristic, DT line*

Drowning – DT line

A drowned DT line is not as serious as it may sound, except that the fish of a lifetime may be lost! Long runs can be expected from fish in a big-fish water, but the danger is that fish will run out and down (or in a sideways curve) and then come up and leap against the weight and drag of the belly of line. Being long and uniformly thick, the line produces sufficient drag to break a weak leader. It is good practice to use fairly strong nylon – 7-pound breaking strain at least. Floating lines are the worst in this respect due to their being the largest diameter, which causes the greatest drag.

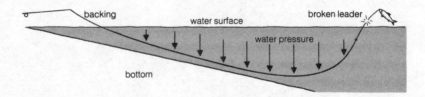

FIGURE 18: *Drowning, DT line*

Backing and fly-line connections – DT line

DT lines, particularly floaters, occupy a lot of a reel's volume, so it is important to have a thin, strong backing to give a safe reserve. A popular but expensive backing is braided Dacron of 18–20 pounds b/s. Any one of several methods of joining line and backing may be used, but if, like me, you feel they are not as versatile and as strong as they might be, you may wish to try my method. I developed it to enable me to change teaching lines quickly, and it involves making loops at the ends of both line and backing then joining them.

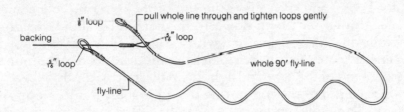

FIGURE 19: *Joining fly-line and backing*

The loop in the line to receive the backing loop is produced as follows:

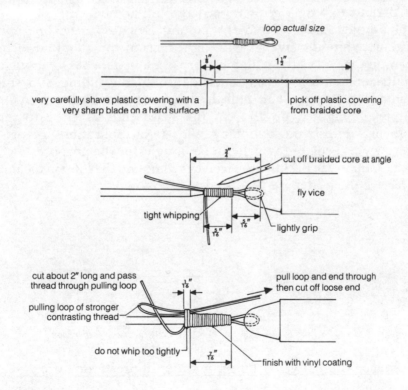

FIGURE 20: *Line to backing loop*

If you do not have one, borrow a fly-vice and obtain a reel of strong fly-tying thread of similar colour to the line, a contrasting stronger thread for the pulling loop, and a bobbin-holder.

Pick or scrape off the plastic covering of the fly-line to expose the braided core, and then shave the end of the covering to a conical shape ⅛ of an inch long down to the core. This should be done carefully on a firm surface and with a scalpel. Now make a loop in the braided core ¾ of an inch long from the inside end of the loop to the large end of the cone and lightly nip the loop in the fly-vice. Cut a 6-inch length of the contrasting thread, double it into a loop and place it to one side, within reach. Put the reel of matching thread in the bobbin-holder, draw off 2 inches of thread and hold this along the loop between the thumb and index finger of your left hand. Starting ⁵⁄₁₆ of an inch from the inside end of the loop, whip tightly for ¼ of an inch, let the bobbin-holder hang, and then cut the spare end of the braided core at an angle, finishing at the large end of the cone.

Continue to whip tightly to the large end of the cone and let the bobbin-holder hang. Hold the pulling loop over the line and continue whipping over it with light tension for ¹⁄₁₆ of an inch. Then cut the end of the whipping thread about 2 inches long while maintaining tension. Pass the cut end through the pulling loop, still maintaining tension, and pull the loop and end back under the whipping. Tighten up and cut the spare end off close to the whipping. Finish the whipping with two applications of proprietary vinyl coating which can be bought for the purpose.

The loop in the backing to receive the line and the loop in the line to receive the leader are produced as follows:

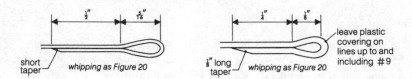

FIGURE 21: *Dacron backing to line loop*   FIGURE 22: *Fly-line to leader loop*

Cheaper alternative backings, in order of preference, are:

- Hollow braided nylon or Terylene of 20 pounds b/s with a ⁵⁄₁₆-inch long loop at the end (*as shown on page 54*) or permanently spliced to the line (*page 53*). These materials are just as good but slightly more bulky than Dacron, and therefore occupy more of the reel's volume.
- Nylon monofilament of 20 pounds b/s permanently joined to the line with a needle knot (*shown on page 52*). While it is

42

smooth and of small diameter, which permits plenty of reserve on the spool, this material never really satisfies me, mainly because the spool centre is always of comparatively small diameter, which causes the nylon to coil. This, in turn, can cause a tangle if the backing goes slack while a fish is being played.

LEADERS

ANYONE LEARNING to cast is destined to spoil a number of leaders while doing so, so it is important not to use anything costly. All that is needed is a 9-foot leader made from three 3-foot lengths of 13-pound, 10-pound and 7-pound b/s nylon knotted together with blood knots, tied thus:

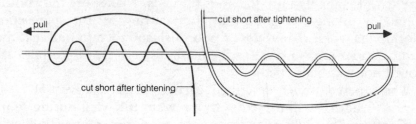

FIGURE 23: *Blood knot*

Having applied spittle to lubricate the turns of nylon, pull both ends steadily to tighten the knot, taking care not to let the nylon cut into any cracks in your fingers. Finally, cut off the spare ends within 1/16 of an inch of the knot.

The 13-pound nylon leader end is attached to the 1/8-of-an-inch line loop by a tucked half-blood knot. When fishing with a floating line, you will probably need to put a small amount of floatant on the loop to prevent it sinking when water creeps up the braided core after entering where the nylon cuts into the plastic covering and adds its weight to the weight of the whipping. All floating-line-to-leader connections suffer in this way, so the floatant treatment is often needed, especially when the retrieve is slow.

The half-blood is used also to attach a fly to the leader, but both it and several alternative knots can leave the leader 'kinked' next to the fly, which causes the fly to be incorrectly aligned and to fish

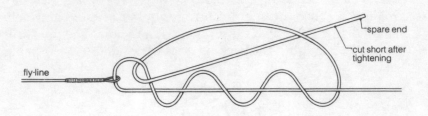

FIGURE 24: *Tucked half-blood knot*

improperly. If you have this problem, then try this method. Tie the knot as small as you can, with a 2-inch spare end. Apply a drop of spittle. Then, while pulling fly and leader gently in opposite directions, hold the spare end in your teeth and at the same time pull towards the fly until the knot tightens. Make sure the knot is sound by giving it a good pull after cutting off the spare end. Nothing is worse than to lose a good fish and then to find that the end of leader looks like a small corkscrew, clearly indicating that your knot was badly tied!

The tapered leader described earlier, or derivatives of it in various lengths, will present a fly or wool tuft well during your early efforts, but when conditions are good, you may well decide to dispense with the taper and use a 9-foot length of level nylon.

Continuously tapered nylon mono leaders are available in various tapers and strengths, but they are comparatively expensive. I find them helpful in windy or very calm conditions, but these are the conditions when you are most likely to find that a 'wind-knot' has accidentally pulled tight. If such a knot cannot be removed, or if it leaves a kink, the leader should be replaced, because its breaking strain is reduced by at least 50 per cent.

Hollow-braided and tapered leaders have become popular of late, but not with me. They are too thick and too conspicuous for my liking – so much so that when one is held up to the light, it is often difficult to see where the line stops and the leader starts.

When your casting has improved to the stage at which you are no longer spoiling many leaders, you may wish to needle-knot a 3-foot length of 13 lb b/s nylon directly to your line, and then blood-knot your leader to this. This makes a neat connection, but you must be ever-vigilant that it does not cut through the line after prolonged use (*see diagram on page 52*).

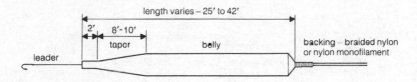

FIGURE 25: *A shooting-head line*

SHOOTING-HEAD LINES AND BACKINGS

I HOPE THE use of the abbreviation ST (for shooting-taper rather than shooting-head) will not be confusing, but this is the term that usually appears in advertisements and on line packaging. A shooting-head can be cut from one end of a DT line and can vary in length from 25 feet for a youth to as much as 42 feet for an expert caster. The length should be chosen to suit the fishing situation and the ability of the caster, but it is always attached to relatively thin, free-sliding backing.

After the basic casting movements and loop-forming action have been learned with a DT line, the 30-foot long #8 ST is the line with which you should learn the method of shooting line. Two problems confront the beginner: becoming accustomed to the 'feel' of the line being separated from the rod-tip by 2–3 feet of backing (called overhang), and holding the thin backing line without letting it slip through the left hand.

ST lines are supreme for long-distance casting, but mainly when some help is given by even the slightest following breeze. However, they do not cast well into a wind, because the thin backing between the bottom rod ring and the ST line does not create sufficient tension in the bottom of the line loop to turn the line over at the end of a long cast. Not to appreciate this only fuels the debate about 'invisible walls' in still conditions. The ST has to rely on its own rolling and forward energy to maintain tension in the top and bottom of the loop while in 'free flight'. As it meets the wind, so forward energy, and therefore tension, is lost, the line crumples and the top of the loop does not turn over and straighten. This problem is more severe with floating ST lines because of their comparatively large diameter and their increased air-resistance. Marginal improvements can be made by using sinking lines, which are smaller in diameter and thus cut through the atmosphere better.

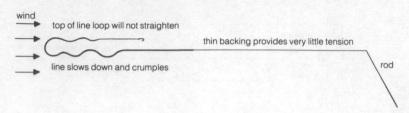

FIGURE 26: *Casting a shooting-head into wind*

The ST must be drawn back for each cast, since the thin backing has insufficient weight to start a loop of rolling energy for a back-cast. However, given the right conditions, and with a #8 line, an average caster should reach from 25–28 yards, including the leader, and a good caster 35 yards plus.

Different circumstances demand different lengths of ST. For instance, the 9-foot #8 rod I described handles 38 feet of #8 shooting-head very well for maximum distance, given an un-obstructed back-cast. However, it is too long for comfort on a reservoir dam, and in this situation a reduction to 30 feet avoids the loss of many flies and the chafing of leaders on the wall top. Lengths of 30–33 feet are also helpful when strong wind blows from behind, since the back-cast is so short, or indeed, given obstructions.

A simple rule of thumb may help in relation to line-weight outside the rod-tip. It is that, given a basic 30-foot length of line of one AFTM number, an extra 4 feet of line of the next lower number is needed to make up the weight difference. For example:

- Total weight of 34 feet of #7 = basic 30 feet of #8
- Total weight of 34 feet of #8 = basic 30 feet of #9

It is important to appreciate also that as the basic line length becomes longer, so the next lower line length increases dis-proportionately to build up the same weight:

Basic line length:	30 feet (10 yards)	36 feet (12 yards)	45 feet (15 yards)	54 feet (18 yards)
Next lower length increase:	4 feet	5 feet	6 feet	7 feet

The method of casting the ST line is very different from that used for the DT. With the ST separated from the rod-tip by 2–3 feet of backing, the whole line is aerialised backwards and forwards, perhaps twice, with easy, controlled rod movements. Then, after the final back-cast, a crisp, fast acceleration is used to propel the ST forward in one long shoot. Having learned the correct technique, many anglers are amazed at the length of shoot they achieve with great economy of effort!

Unfortunately, I have detected a certain amount of prejudice against the shooting-head, particularly among anglers with long experience or traditional attitudes. This is rather sad, because there are good uses for this line. The greatest, in relation to people, is perhaps its use by anglers with debilitating medical conditions. Those suffering from arthritis, rheumatism and tennis elbow can achieve good fishing distances with minimum effort!

However good the splice between the backing and ST line, the joint always catches slightly when it is drawn through the rod rings, particularly when these are made of wire. This is sometimes a source of irritation, especially during a slow retrieve or when very gentle offers are being felt for. And as nylon backing cannot be held satisfactorily in the hand during a figure-of-eight retrieve, a line-tray is essential.

Shooting-head length

What governs the choice of length of an ST line? To answer this question fully would need a thesis, but in simple terms the answer depends on ability and circumstance. Beginners must start with a length which they can manage comfortably. In practical terms, this means 26 feet for youths and women, and usually 30 feet for adult males. The 'expert' will also find 30 feet an easy length to remove from the water when he uses a very fast-sinking line and where the back-cast is restricted.

The moderately experienced angler will find that a 33-foot length increases casting distance, and the experienced caster will derive a further increase with 35 feet. Expert casters using 38 feet or even 42 feet will cast very long distances, but only when they use the double-haul technique. Of course, each increase in length produces a heavier line and, therefore, the potential for greater distance, given the right rod and technique.

Casting distance is significantly related to the length of the ST line. Bearing in mind the flexible-weight concept, it is not reasonable to expect it to travel through the air like a javelin once it has straightened. A strong wind from behind will allow the line to 'sit' on the wind, but this assistance is limited. A good cast, whatever the distance or conditions, relies on the tensions created by the rolling and forward energy of the loop to maintain an effective line profile throughout its flight. Ideally, the line should straighten just above the water after all forward motion has ceased. So for a very long cast, the line will be in the air for a comparatively long time, and the only factor that will extend the time taken for the loop to straighten, in flight, is an increase in the length of the line. For the longest fishing casts of between 40 and 50 yards, ST line lengths of between 38 and 42 feet are needed.

Side-wind – ST line

The ST does not perform well in a strong side-wind, particularly if the bank-to-fly distance is the measure of success. Again, it is the 'free flight' nature of this line which causes the difficulty. If an ST is cast square across the wind, the heavy belly of the shooting-head starts to drive well, but as the forward impetus slows down, so the top part of the loop is blown progressively downwind as it tries to turn over. Towards the end of the cast only the thinner down-taper of the line is trying to straighten, and this, being lighter, is blown further downwind. Viewed from above, the ST will be angled sideways with a large curve taking the down-taper and leader parallel to the bank. In these conditions a DT line is a much better proposition.

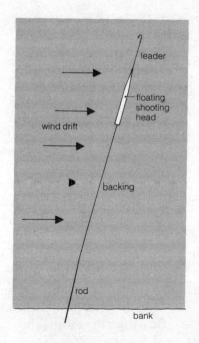

FIGURE 27: *Side drift, ST line*

Side drift – ST floating line

A floating ST line behaves fairly well in a side-wind, since the head, provided it is not too long, travels at the surface current speed without much influence from the thin backing. If slightly greased, the backing will float and tend not to submerge its splice with the floating line. However, this backing should not be used with a rod intended for use with a slow-sinking line. The grease is transferred via the rod rings to the line, which will then refuse to sink in places. In a one-rod situation the rings should be thoroughly cleaned with detergent during the change-over.

Sinking characteristic – ST line

The shooting-head is ideal for fishing from a sloping wall or bank so typical of reservoirs, particularly early in the season when lines of various sinking rates are used. The head sinks near to the bottom, but the backing does not. After a pre-determined sinking period, the first part of the retrieve straightens the backing, and then the ST is drawn back parallel to the bottom, not into it.

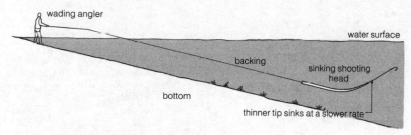

FIGURE 28: *Sinking characteristic, ST line*

Early season trout fishing is often difficult because the fish are in deep water, well out from the bank. For me, half the pleasure of fishing is to help inexperienced anglers to catch fish, and, as might be imagined, the early season is the most difficult time. This is unfortunate, because the newcomers arrive at the waterside so full of optimism, but often without the casting ability to deal with the problems.

One situation which I remember well concerned a husband-and-wife team who had decided to take up fishing before retirement. We were fishing a pleasant two-lake fishery and the lady had left her husband to come over to the lake I was fishing. My strategy that day was to cast a 38-foot #8 fast-sinking ST with a 9-foot 7- pound leader and a size 12 Teal Blue and Silver fly about 40 yards out. The fish were feeding from 15 to 20 feet down, and I had caught several. As the bank was grassy and the wind light, from behind, I let the braided nylon backing fall on to the bank, although a line-tray would have been necessary in any other situation. I was landing a fish when the lady arrived and her comments made it plain that she had caught nothing in three visits. That was when the fun started! I cast my line and passed my rod to her. After letting the line sink for what she described as 'an eternity', she started to draw in and had a 1½-pound rainbow almost immediately. This happened five times more in the next half an hour. Her husband was amazed. He had had not so much as an offer! We never did 'let on'.

Drowning, – ST line

The thin, light backing used with an ST line can be drawn through the water smoothly in any direction. Also, the short line has greatly reduced water drag, so the risk of leader breakage or the hook tearing out is greatly reduced.

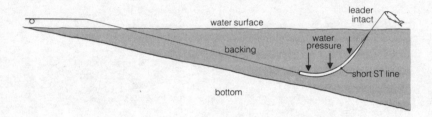

FIGURE 29: *Drowning, ST line*

One unforgettable warm May evening at Chew, trout were starting to rise about 45 yards out, so I decided to go for nearly maximum distance with a 36-foot #8 floating ST and a size 12 Olive Midge Pupa on a 10-foot leader tapered to 6 pounds. A gentle breeze was blowing from left to right as I waded quietly out with a line-tray attached to my belt. My first cast was about 25 yards, and I allowed the line simply to drift round in an arc to the right. Nothing happened. For the next cast I pulled off some more backing and gave extra acceleration to propel the fly out to about 33 yards. My fly had just started to drift round, helped by a gentle retrieve, when it was taken savagely. The fish went down into a searing run straight out for about 40 yards and then jumped twice. I could do nothing to stop it. One touch on the screeching reel would have broken the leader instantly. After I had carefully played the fish back to short range, it made three lesser runs before I could net it. This aquatic athlete was a rainbow weighing an ounce under 4 pounds, and it had the largest fins and tail, proportionately, that I have seen.

This story merely draws attention to the need for plenty of backing, particularly on large waters, which is where these super-fit trout are often encountered. The effect of leader breakage when a short length of backing comes to an end is devastating! I am convinced, too, that this particular trout would have broken the leader with its first jump against a drowned line of any other type, so the ST was a wise choice, apart from being needed for distance casting.

Backing – ST line

Being, at most, 50 per cent of the length of a DT line for fishing purposes, the ST leaves a lot more room for backing on the reel spool than does a full DT. Be prepared for this, and buy enough backing in a continuous length to fill the reel (*see page 31*).

Another advantage with an ST line is that the line can be wound in more rapidly, a not insignificant point when a particularly lively fish is being played. The reason is that the backing, being thin, does not reduce its diameter as quickly as a plastic-covered line does when unwound from the spool and it also starts, at the line splice, with a larger diameter underneath it.

The two types of backing I recommend for use with shooting-heads are 20-pound nylon monofilament or braided nylon of 20–25 pounds b/s. The mono slides through rod rings freely and is best for the longest casts, but it is prone to tangling. Braided nylon, being a little less smooth, reduces casting distance slightly but does not tangle because of its greater diameter and flexibility. I believe it is preferable to use 20-pound braided backing for #6 and 7 lines with a reel spool of up to 3½ inches diameter, and 25-pound for heavier lines and larger reels. A useful tip is to use white backing for dark lines and black for light-coloured lines, the contrast being of help in judging the overhang.

The joining of nylon monofilament to the ST or leaders to all types of line demands a needle knot, which is tied as on page 52.

Some people find difficulty in tying this knot because it is positioned close to the end of the line and, because of the springiness of the nylon, the turns do not always maintain their correct positions. If you experience problems, try the following method.

Push the nylon through the hole and start to form the knot 2–3

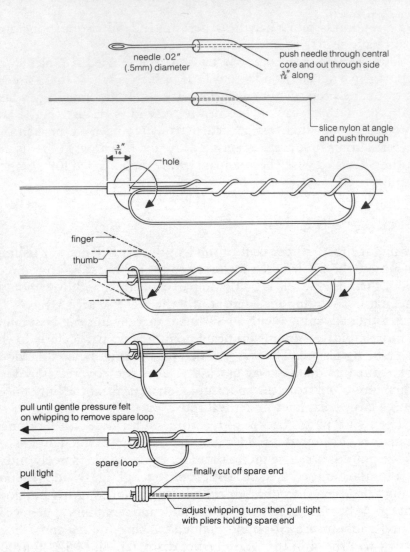

FIGURE 30: *Needle knot*

inches along the line. When twisting the nylon around the line, hold each successive turn between the thumb and first finger of your left hand. This means you are working blind, so to speak, but the twists will be positioned neatly.

Now remove the spare nylon loop by pulling the nylon through the line, and then pull the short end. These two pulls should be enough to maintain the shape of the knot. Finally, slide the knot down the line until it is level with the hole, pull the nylon through the line in stages, tighten and cut off the spare end.

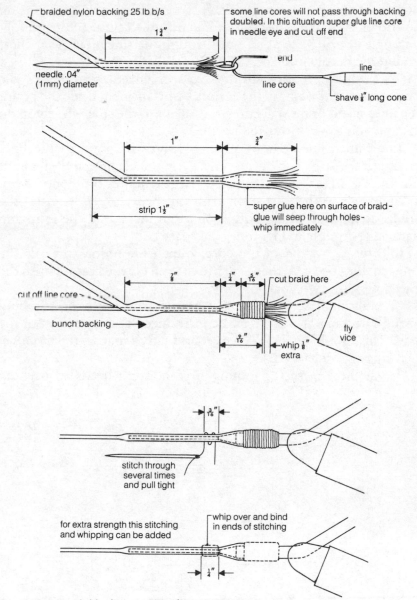

FIGURE 31: *Braided backing to ST splice*

Hollow braided nylon can be joined to an ST by a splice. This has the advantage of sliding smoothly through the rod rings (due to its gradual build-up of diameter) but it is permanent. The same splice can be used to join hollow-weave Terylene backing to DT and WF lines, and it is made as follows.

Remove 1½ inches of plastic covering from the thick end of the shooting-head, and carefully 'shave' an ⅛-of-an-inch long cone on the end of the plastic. Insert a needle into the centre of the hollow backing and bring the point out through the side after 1¾ inches, leaving the needle in place.

Pass the line core through the eye of the needle and pull needle and core until the point of the cone is ¾-of-an-inch inside the braid. The needle and braid will come out through the side while you do this and you can remove the needle.

Now Superglue a ³⁄₁₆ of an inch length of braid to the line, starting at the large end of the cone. Grip the backing in a vice and, starting ¹⁄₁₆ of an inch from the large end of the cone, whip ⁵⁄₁₆ of an inch as the glue sets. Trim off the nylon ends, insert the pulling loop, and whip another ⅛ of an inch. Pull the loop and spare end through and trim off the spare end.

Hold the spare end of the core, bunch the nylon towards the cone, cut the core, and then pull the core inside the braid. Finish the whipping with two coats of vinyl.

For additional strength, a ³⁄₁₆-of-an-inch length of stitching through backing and core can be introduced at the bottom of the cone. This should be whipped over and vinyl-coated. (*For details of the whipping, see page 41.*)

The method I use for joining my shooting-heads to backing

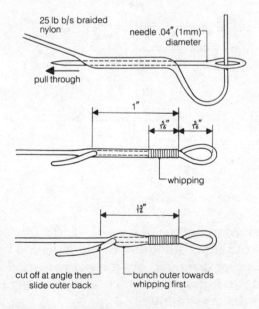

FIGURE 32: *Loop for hollow braided nylon and Terylene backing*

Hanningfield Reservoir – the writer enjoying himself at a casting show and clinic, demonstrating in rough conditions. Also note the well equipped lodge and convenient car park

Chigborough Fishery – a very comfortable lake with clear banks which make casting easy. Casting platforms and rowing boats are provided. Note the good water level in spite of a long drought
(Photos: Tom Charlton)

4. Rod hand has moved another three inches and stopped abruptly. Rod handle tilts forwards. Wrist angle closed slightly. Rod starts to recoil and straighten pulling the line very quickly

3. Rod hand smoothly accelerating and nearly fully forward. Rod has maximum bend from line weight and line starts to move forwards. Rod handle vertical. Wrist angle unchanged

A thirty-five yard shooting-head cast. Note: the sequence shows rod hand moving parallel to dam wall top throughout cast

8. Hand static. Wrist angle closed, lowering rod-tip slightly, but it is still high. Very fast, narrow loop speeds away

at about ten degrees above horizontal

7. Rod hand static. Wrist angle closes lowering rod-tip slightly. Rod straight. Rolling and pulling line loop forms

2. Body and rod hand move forwards. Rod starts to bend against line weight. Rod handle still tilted back. Wrist angle unchanged

1. Compared to the DT cast between pages 86 and 87 the ST (or WF) line needs a shorter rod-hand movement. The line straightens backwards. Rod hand moves back just behind head and rod-tip 'drifts' back. Body leans back slightly

6. Rod hand static. Rod finishes recoil forwards and rod-tip dips slightly. Line continues to move forwards at a higher level. Note: the amount the rod-tip dips dictates the width of line loop produced, which can be varied

5. Rod hand static. Rod continues to recoil and straighten

(Photos: Ken Lynch)

Loch-style fishing – in an ideal ripple. These anglers
are sitting on plank seats and raising their rod-tips
high to bring their flies to the surface

Returning a specimen brown trout to the water
unharmed. There is a growing interest in the use of
barbless hooks and catch-and-release game fishing

(Photos: Peter Gathercole)

allows me to change them quickly when necessary. I start by producing a loop on the ST (*see page 41*) and a loop in the hollow nylon as shown opposite. I then join two loops as for the DT to its backing. This join does not slide through the rod rings as smoothly as a splice, but it is more versatile.

The best all-round performance will be achieved with oxide-lined rings, in terms of both casting distance and freedom from wear, and both types of nylon backing can be used with them with confidence. Wire rings, however, need more consideration. I do not use braided backing with these rings, as any small particles of grit trapped in the weave quickly form small grooves in the wire. Nylon mono will not harm wire rings, provided it is kept clean, but I use it only with bridge rings. My experience with snake rings is not so happy, in that, with persistent double-hauling, the nylon eventually cuts through the whippings holding the rings!

Leaders – ST line

Because of its 'free-flight' characteristic and the unavoidable minor variations in casting performance, the ST line turns the leader over inconsistently. A following wind helps, as does braking the final part of the shoot (*see page 36*), but at the expense of distance. If you strive for 100 per cent presentation, then, I am sad to say, with an ST line you must expect permanent under-achievement!

The leader recommended for the DT line will perform well for your first efforts, but do check regularly for accidental wind-knots 'tied' in casting.

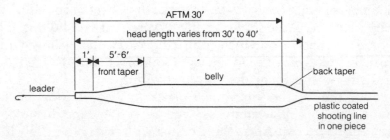

FIGURE 33: *A weight-forward line*

WEIGHT-FORWARD (WF) LINES AND BACKINGS

A WEIGHT-FORWARD (or forward-taper) line is, to all intents and purposes, a shooting-head, except that the head is manufactured in one piece with its shooting-line. The totally smooth join between the head and shooting-line is a great advantage when such a line is fished slowly while you feel for gentle takes. The same freedom from 'clicks' in the rod rings is also good when a large fish, hooked on a light leader, makes one last, despairing run. The 'built-in' shooting line of plastic-coated core also handles better than mono or braided nylon.

The length of the WF head varies considerably, depending on make or type of line. It is important to check the length before purchase, because a beginner will find a length of 30–33 feet satisfactory, whereas an experienced caster will need 36 feet or more for better distance. Line-life will be extended if you contrive to cast with the thicker part of the back-taper in the tip-ring, rather than the thin shooting line, the covering of which tends to break up if the line is used regularly in this way.

Because the shooting-line is made from the same material as the head, with a gently tapering blend between the two, difficulty may be experienced at first in judging the right amount of line to have outside the rod-tip. It is easier with a floating line, because a significant difference is apparent between the belly and shooting-line diameters. Average figures are 0.064 inches and 0.040 inches respectively for a WF #8 floating line. For a WF #8 extra-fast-sinking line, the figures are 0.047 inches and 0.037 inches diameter – a very different proposition!

The solution to the problem is to set up the rod and line in a suitable open space, assume a normal casting position with the rod horizontal and with the back-taper of the line 3 feet or so within the tip-ring, and mark the shooting-line where you will hold it. This can be done with a one-inch-long ring of lacquer paint, which eventually will wear off. Do not use a volatile, quick-drying paint, because this will damage the plastic covering.

Because the WF shooting-line is plastic-coated, it does not slide through the rod rings quite as well as nylon, and distance is somewhat restricted. An average caster will manage 20–23 yards, and a good caster 27 yards plus, including leader. Oxide-lined rod rings will help to produce longer casts than are possible with wire rings, particularly with double-hauling, although the difference will not be great. Oxide rings definitely feel smoother on the retrieve, which helps in the detection of gentle offers.

The WF line seems to be the least understood by anglers in so far as head-length and method of casting are concerned. To say that head-length matters is an understatement! Of three manufacturers whose products I know really well, one used to make a 30-foot length but has recently increased it to 33 feet; the second has always made lines of 36 feet; and the third, lines of 40 feet – all in #8. Clearly, only an expert can aerialise a 40-foot head-length, yet thousands are sold to less experienced fishermen.

I well remember one experienced angler who wanted to improve his casting and had said despairingly on the telephone: 'The longer the distance I try to cast, the worse my style becomes.' When he arrived, we started by using my rod and DT line and after an hour spent correcting the usual faults, he was casting well, so I was intrigued when he said: 'I won't be able to do that with my rod and line!' Having put his outfit together, I asked him to demonstrate. Sure enough, as his line extended on the third shoot, it just crumpled in mid-air. But it transpired that the DT line he imagined he was using was a slow-sinking WF with a 33-foot head-length which had been put in the wrong box. Once I had discovered the reason, and had shown him how to position the head just outside the rod-tip and cast it with one long, final shoot, he was delighted with the result. I have dealt with many similar situations.

Another aspect arises when the head-length is 40 feet, a length which few anglers can aerialise properly. For an average caster wanting a shorter length, the answer to the problem is to treat the long WF head as a partial DT line, while capitalising on the benefits of the WF. The disadvantage of the DT line for distance-casting is the weight and thickness of the belly sliding through the rod rings, whereas the WF shooting-line is thinner and slides more freely. With this in mind, it is better to cast the long WF head in the following manner:

Having lifted the line from the water, cast it forwards twice, shooting enough line to take 36–37 feet outside the rod-tip. Then, on the third and final forward cast, release the line completely as if it were an ST. The thinner shooting-line will eventually come into the rod rings, slide well and produce a much longer final shoot than would a DT. This assumes, of course, that conditions are suitable for the use of ST or WF lines.

I remember when ideal conditions for the use of the WF line occurred for days on end at Ardleigh Reservoir, when a light, early summer breeze prevailed from the west along my favourite bank. During the evenings the trout were feeding in the surface film, heading slowly up the breeze.

Because the water was quite shallow, I found it necessary to wade out about 5 yards, so I decided to use a line-tray to hold my retrieved line. I could have dropped my line on the water, but it would have floated a long way sideways due to the speed of drift and the time taken over a slow retrieve. This, in turn, would have caused a significant resistance when I came to re-cast. My method was to cast a 33-feet long WF #8 floating head straight across or slightly down the drift and then retrieve my size 12 Pheasant Tail Nymph very slowly. After retrieving until the thicker line had reached my hand, and drawing the line straight off the water into the back-cast, I shot 3½ yards of line on the first forward cast to position the head outside the rod-tip. Keeping the line in the air, I made another back-cast, following it with a final shoot of 12–14 yards to complete the casting sequence.

I could expect offers anywhere from 10 to 20 yards out from the rod-tip and I could feel them precisely. The easy handling quality of the shooting-line, together with an absence of unnatural drift of the head and freedom from 'ST ring-clicking', ensured most comfortable fishing. I felt little concern for the 6-pound b/s leader in relation to the quite large fish present because the light head ensured that it wouldn't be drowned.

I had several mixed limits of brown and rainbow trout up to 4 pounds each in those happy evenings. The experience was made the more pleasant by the thought that my choice of line had made such a contribution.

Side drift, sinking and drowning characteristics – WF lines

The floating WF line behaves in similar manner to the ST, except that the shooting-line drifts faster because of its greater diameter. Good judgement is needed to decide when the floating shooting-line is being influenced by the wind sufficiently to drag the fly at an unnatural speed. The choice then is to change to a larger fly (which would imitate a bigger food item that would naturally move more quickly), to an ST (which would drift more slowly), or to a very slow-sinking line (which would be less influenced by the wind).

The thin shooting-line of a sinking WF line sinks quite well, so its effect lies between the characteristics of DT and ST lines. A sinking WF is generally more appropriate when fished from a steeply sloping bank, whereas the ST is a better choice for a gently sloping one.

The drowning effect is, again, between the DT's and ST's. In theory, therefore, a slightly finer leader and smaller fly could be used than would be used with a DT line, but I would not take the risk.

Backing for WF lines

The alternatives are exactly the same as those described for the DT line. However, the WF shooting-line is thinner than the DT's for a significant length, so it occupies less of the reel's capacity, providing room for a safer reserve.

Leaders for WF lines

The leader described for the DT line should be used at first, and presentation should be better than that described for the ST. This is because the plastic-covered shooting-line causes additional friction in the rod rings, and therefore slightly more tension in the bottom of the line loop, which helps 'turn-over'.

——— *LINE DIAMETERS AND* ——— *CASTING PERFORMANCE*

Type of line	Belly diameter of DT 8 line – inches	Percentage of floating line diameter
Floating	0.061	100
Neutral-density	0.058	95
Medium-sinking	0.052	85
Fast-sinking	0.048	79

The diameter of a line has a large bearing on what one might describe as its 'castability'. With this in mind, I have tabulated the approximate belly diameters of the different types of DT line, all rated #8 by the same maker. They all have the same weight per AFTM 30 feet whether they are whole DT lines, shooting-heads or weight-forward heads. Slight differences may occur in the manufacturing tolerances of various makers' lines.

In extreme conditions, when top performance can make the difference between good sport and none, it is important to use the 'line for the job'. At other times any line can be used, chosen on the basis of personal preference in relationship to prevailing conditions.

A floating line, having the greatest diameter, offers most air-resistance at the front of the line loop. This is most noticeable in 'dead-air' conditions, when it is more difficult to make the loop straighten at long range. In this situation a greased neutral-density line, having a slightly smaller diameter, may straighten better when a floating line is needed. Given a strong wind from behind, the larger diameter of the floating line will 'fly' on the wind well and have its loop blown straight. However, a complication arises in obtaining a good back-cast, which has to be straightened into the wind. Again, a neutral-density may help and a medium-sinker definitely will. In fact, for maximum distance in a strong following wind, the medium-sinker probably performs best. A fast-sinker penetrates best into a strong wind because of its small diameter, but it may hit the water fairly hard as a result of this ability to cut through the air-stream. A medium-sinker does not penetrate quite as well, but gives a better presentation.

It is as well also to examine the casting performance of a sink-tip line. This has 10–20 feet of sinking line 'built on' to the tip end of a floating line, and is ideal for use in certain conditions. However, in casting, and because of the different line densities, the tip end seems to 'flip over' at the ends of the forward and backward line extensions. Experienced anglers are able to compensate for this without difficulty, but a beginner would do well to wait until he has developed a good degree of line control before using this type of line.

Practical Casting

---------- TACKLE FOR BEGINNERS ----------

HAVING READ the preceding rather technical chapters, the new-comer will be wondering how, in Heaven's name, he is going to sort out what he needs. So, to save time and trouble, here is the ideal list of equipment which the beginner needs to start casting, though for fishing he will need also waterproofs, a landing-net, flies and other items listed in the chapter on tackle (*page 181*):

- One 9-foot #8 carbon rod, one 3⅝ inches diameter reel and two spare spools.
- One DT #8 medium-sinking line with Dacron, hollow-weave Terylene or hollow braided nylon backing.
- One ST #8 fast-sinking line 30 feet long and an appropriate length of 25-pound b/s white hollow braided nylon backing.
- One WF #8 floating line with a 33-foot head-length and backing as for the DT line. (*For line-colour, see page 163.*)
- Spools of 13-pound, 10-pound and 7-pound nylon to make 9-foot leaders; darning-wool for tufts, and two dull-coloured tennis sweat bands.

Should your budget be limited, or should you expect not to fish much, you can do quite well with the following outfit:

- One 9-foot #8 glass-fibre rod, with one 3⅝ inches diameter reel and one spare spool.
- One DT #8 floating line and backing (as above).
- One ST #8 medium-sinking line 30 feet long and an appropriate length of 25-pound white hollow braided nylon backing.
- Nylon, wool and sweat bands as above.

- Whip loops on the backing ends and leader ends of the DT, ST and WF lines (*as shown on pages 41 and 42*).

It is important from a progressive learning point of view to produce your shooting-head in a certain way. Shop around until you find a whole DT #8 fast- or medium-sinking line at an economy price. These are advertised in angling magazines and are good value for a beginner to start with. Cut off the first 30 feet and then three pieces of belly 3 feet 3 inches long. The remainder will be made into your fishing ST line later, when you have decided what length suits you after learning to cast well.

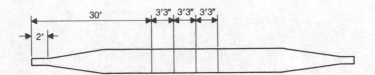

FIGURE 34: *Cutting a training shooting-head*

Make sure the front end parallel portion is only 2 feet long. If it is longer, cut it down to the correct length before cutting the 30-foot shooting-head. Make the usual ⅛-inch loop at the leader end and ⁵⁄₁₆-inch loops on the seven ends of the 30-foot and short belly lengths (*as shown on pages 41 and 42*). Alternatively, you can loop the ST only at first, then loop up the belly lengths when needed, because to do the whole job at once will take a long time. Keep the three 3-foot looped belly lengths in a plastic envelope ready to add length to the ST when you come to practise. It is important that a piece which is added is joined to the thick backing end of the ST, not the thin leader end.

Now make ⁵⁄₁₆-inch loops in the ends of the Dacron backing (if used) (*as shown on page 42*) and ⁵⁄₁₆-inch loops in the hollow backing (*as shown on page 54*). Finally, join the lines to the appropriate backing (*as shown on page 41*).

Knot on 9-foot long leaders of 7-pound nylon to your lines and add wool tufts made from single pieces of darning wool 1¼ inches long, knotting the nylon in the centre of each piece with a tucked half-blood knot. Should you prefer something a little more elaborate, that will turn over better, make up tapered leaders (*as described on page 43*).

Push the two sections of rod together with the rod rings in line, attach the reel positioned for left-hand wind, having previously added the reel spool with the DT #8 line. Pull some line from the reel and thread the leader through the rod rings, then bring the 'wool-fly' back to your hand and hold it; otherwise the line, being heavy, will run down the rings. You are now ready to start casting!

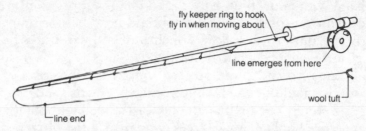

FIGURE 35: *Rod assembled*

FIRST EFFORTS

THREE BASIC FACTORS about learning to cast well must be remembered at all times.

Practise your casting on grass. This will do no harm, since most of your casting while fishing will be with the line extending over the water. It is a delusion to believe that you will be thinking about casting at the waterside – you will be concentrating on fishing.

Casting development is a process of 'two steps forward and one step backward', so be prepared! The reality is that you learn one aspect well, and then spoil it when you try to learn the next stage. Casting entails moving quickly, and you cannot think of everything at once. Don't try to progress too quickly when things go wrong. Revert to what you can do well, practise it again, and then have another try at the next stage.

Check your hand and rod positions frequently. Literally, stop casting at random to see the position you are in. Be prepared for a few surprises! The line will fall to the ground, of course, but this will do no harm. Just straighten it and start again.

Now find yourself an unobstructed area of grass about 100 feet square and position yourself in the centre, with the wind, if any, blowing from left to right to keep the line away from the rod.

Put the rod down on the grass pointing in the direction selected for the forward cast and with the reel handle facing upwards. Draw out 27–28 feet of line from the rod-tip (with the leader adding to this length) and lay it on the grass.

Slip the two sweat bands, one on top of the other, on your right wrist and under the sleeve of any clothing. Hold the rod in your right hand with your 'thumb up the rod' in the most comfortable position you can find. The bands should now be positioned far enough up your arm to allow 2 inches of rod extension behind the reel to be slipped underneath them. Some rods have sharp-edged fittings, so check and protect your wrist if necessary. The sweat bands should be used while you both practise and fish until you are absolutely certain that you can cast as well without them as with. You need only a few degrees of angular wrist movement to cast really well, and the sweat bands will allow just the right amount. As a test, remove one sweat band first, to make comparisons.

Grip the line against the cork handle with the index finger of the right hand and pull off another 6–7 feet of line from the reel and let it hang down, but do not release the right finger grip. Now lightly grip the line between thumb and index finger of your left hand, level with your trouser pocket. Raise your right hand to the level of your ear, letting the line slide through your left-hand grip. Turn the line once round your left hand and, still gripping the line with your thumb and index finger, tuck your hand in your left trouser pocket. (A left-hand coat pocket will do just as well.) Should you not follow this procedure, you will find the left hand rising and tending to follow the rod, and you will have an irritating tendency to let the line go just when you do not want to. In this way, your line is firmly trapped in a position where it can be forgotten. Release the right index finger grip and, correctly done, you will find the line length outside the rod-tip unaltered at about 28 feet.

Take up the foot positions shown on page 21, with your left foot parallel to the direction in which the line is to travel. This alignment helps anyone who tends to turn on the spot while casting. Now place your right hand in the fully forward position 'along the cane', with the rod angled forwards at 20 degrees from the vertical, which should cause the line to hang forward and then lie along the ground.

Turn the rod-tip out 15 degrees to the right to make a continuous line through the forearm to the left foot (as shown on page 21).

Remembering your practice with paint-brush and water, accelerate your rod-arm in a level plane backwards, give your wrist a little backward flick, stop it abruptly just behind your head, then watch the line straighten out of the corner of your eye. Without letting the line drop behind, accelerate the rod forwards, flick and stop abruptly in the fully-forward position. Let the line straighten and fall to the ground.

Say to yourself: '*Pull, flick, w – a – i – t, push, flick, w – a – i – t*', to achieve the correct timing.

Repeat this sequence several times until you can maintain the right acceleration, flick and abrupt stop that makes the line speed backwards and forwards with minimum effort. Now have a rest, because your arm muscles will be tense.

Before starting again, adjust your position slightly in any area where you are not perfectly comfortable. The diagrams are for general guidance only. They do not allow for individual physical variations.

Try another sequence of casts, making sure that your hand, and therefore the rod-tip, is travelling in a substantially level plane. This ensures that the bottom of the line loop travels parallel to the ground.

Another way of thinking about accelerating the rod-tip is to imagine a small piece of mud stuck loosely to the rod-tip but which you want to start moving along and then flick off at the last

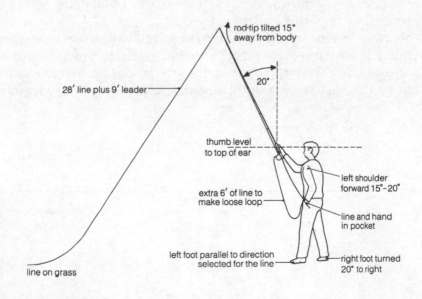

FIGURE 36: *Starting position*

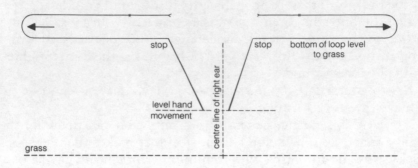

FIGURE 37: *Correct hand movement*

moment, level with the ground and as far as possible. This, of course, applies to both back-cast and forward cast. No force is needed, just a steady build–up to a fast speed and then an abrupt stop.

If, as often happens, you use too much force, the rod will be pushed downwards at the end of the arm movement. This 'chopping down' comes from the forearm, and but for the sweat bands could come from the wrist. The effect is to cause the bottom of the loop to travel downward and the loop to become too large, so restricting casting distance. The rod-tip seldom pulls 4 ounces of dynamic weight during a cast, so there is little point in trying to put more effort than this into a cast!

It takes a split-second for your eye to tell your brain to instruct your hand to move, which very much affects the problem of deciding when to start the forward cast. The right moment is as the line end is seen to have a slight upward curve. By the time you have

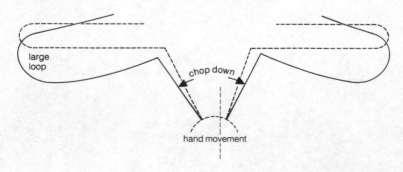

FIGURE 38: *Incorrect hand movement*

reacted, it will be straight. Should you leave it until the line is visually straight, it will be dropping before you react. If you come forward while the line still has a loop in it, you will be reminded by a sharp crack and the possible loss of the leader end! This applies equally to the forward cast.

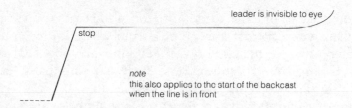

FIGURE 39: *Correct moment to start forward cast*

The next stage is to cast backwards and forwards several times without stopping. Try to get a rhythm going, so that the line is extending crisply without too much effort on your part. *Make sure the rod does the work.* At this point you may notice ripples developing in the line as you cast. These are caused by uneven hand acceleration and can be prevented by a smoother build-up of speed.

Practise the hand-stopping procedure to check positions at random, and let the line fall to the ground at the extreme forward and backward extensions to check that the two are in line. The positions should be along the previously selected imaginary line parallel with the line through the left foot. If the alignment is wrong, then probably you have forgotten about moving the hand 'along the cane'. This is caused by not remembering the feeling of the hand moving away from you going forward and being pushed inward on the way back. If you allow natural instinct to prevail, misalignment will be the result.

Another common problem is to cast the line across your front and back which is caused by rotating the shoulders.

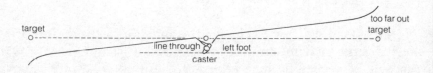

FIGURE 40: *Misaligned cast: hand across front and out behind*

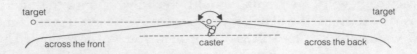

FIGURE 41: *Misaligned cast: shoulder rotation*

A good place to practise the alignment of the casts is on a sports field, where you can cast along one of the white lines. You will notice any error immediately you let your fly-line fall to the ground. Failing this, three markers, such as tennis balls, can be placed in line and you can cast over these.

Try another continuous sequence of casts and have a good look at the loop as it extends. It should be tilted away from you at the same 15-degree angle as the rod, which is a great advantage. The top of the loop, leader and wool 'fly' will be to the right and outside the rod-tip. Should the leader end drop, as it inevitably will while you are fishing, it will not tangle with the line or rod. Furthermore, the top of the loop, being further away, is easier to see when you turn your head to watch the back-cast.

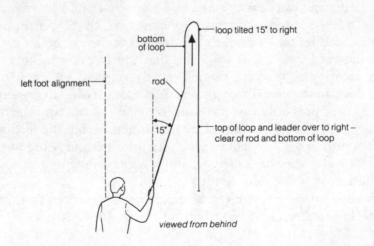

FIGURE 42: *Advantage of tilting rod*

Understanding how to change the angle of cast is an important step towards total line control. A high back-cast and a low forward cast will be needed frequently in actual fishing. They are achieved by hand movements similar to those made when you tilted the back of the cane upwards. Remember, the forward movement, although lower, is still subject to the feeling of the hand moving away from you. But, because the back-cast movement is high, it does not feel pushed towards you. Since this movement feels easier, more care must be taken to keep the hand movement straight and under control.

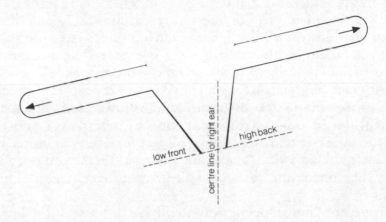

FIGURE 43: *Low forward cast, high back-cast*

Take your right hand along a line tilted upwards by about 15 degrees, with your thumb still passing level with the top of your ear. The length of arm movement and the method of acceleration are exactly the same as for the level cast, except that the plane is tilted. Try several consecutive back-casts and forward casts to get the rhythm, then stop on the forward extension and let the line fall the short distance to the grass. If the line does not extend well, remember the paint-brush and water flicking exercise and movements.

Make another sequence of casts and stop your hand movement in several places to check that it is where it should be. Don't worry if you are a little awry to start with – you will soon correct yourself once you see the flaws. Indeed, you will be surprised how quickly you will diagnose your own faults.

Have another rest. In spite of the light weight of the rod and line, your muscular tension will be quite significant, due largely to your gripping the rod handle too tightly and to the unaccustomed arm action. Even experienced anglers find this when they learn a new way of casting.

You've probably guessed the next thing to be practised. Yes, the high forward and low back-casting. And to do it, you merely reverse the tilt.

Practise with the 28-foot length of line until you can change the angle of cast at will during a casting sequence. Once you have achieved this fluency, you will develop a confidence that puts you in control of events, and which you will need for the next steps. And always remember that it's a good idea to take frequent rests.

Pull out another 3 feet of line and repeat the whole procedure. When you can control this length, add another 3 feet, and so on until you cannot comfortably manage any more. The manageable length of line is usually 38 to 40 feet, and at no stage should you try to cast a line which is too long and makes you try too hard. Keep a good style and extra distance will follow. Remember the 'Marshall-one-yard-less rule': cast one yard less than you can manage and style will be good; go all-out for one yard more, and the result will be awful! The strange thing is that if you obey the rule, your maximum distance will grow progressively, almost unnoticed.

Notice how much longer you now have to wait for the line to straighten. It seems an eternity. Also, a very crisp flick and a positive stop are needed to extend the line, not more force.

You should practise one more part of the basic rod action as preparation for increasing your casting distance, because with a longer line in the air, you will need extra rod movement to control it.

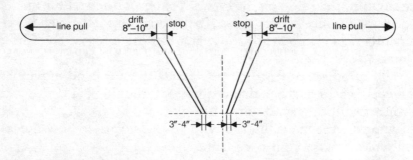

FIGURE 44: *Extra rod movement*

Having made your usual hand movement, and stopped the rod, watch the line extending and, while it is still pulling, 'drift' your hand gently backwards or forwards 3 – 4 inches more and so tilt the rod-tip from 8–10 inches. The movement must not be so fast as to let the line slacken, and under no circumstances must this rod-tip travel be treated as part of the acceleration process. If it were, it would throw the line downwards and open up the loop. But this little extra movement will help to straighten out any slight ripples in the line and to get the longer line moving smoothly while you cast in either direction.

Never allow shoulder swing to develop, particularly as you make the 'drift'. Shoulder swing ruins the straightness and alignment in casting that I try so hard to create, and the result is pure frustration. I well remember George, who came to me self-taught, saying he was fed up with the tangles and muddles he got into when trying for extra distance. Well, George is one of Nature's gentlemen, 5 feet 7 inches tall and built like the original 'brick shed'. One look at his casting was enough – too much strength, not enough speed and a great big shoulder swing coming all the way from his knees!

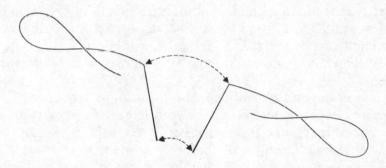

FIGURE 45: *Effect of shoulder swing*

Having corrected the first two problems, I found that, because of his arm length and breadth of shoulder, he could not easily stop the swing. However, the solution was amazingly simple. Instead of positioning his feet in the usual way – left foot in the direction of cast, right foot to the right, behind, turned out 20 degrees – I asked him to turn his toes gently inwards as much as possible. After shuffling his feet into the most comfortable position possible, bearing in mind the strange feeling of his new 'foundation', he found a revolution (no pun intended) about to break. It was almost impossible for him to swing from his knees, his shoulders

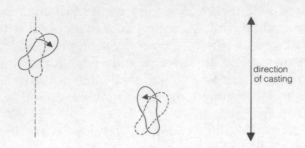

FIGURE 46: *Turn toes inward*

maintained the correct position, and he was delighted! Not long afterwards, he was casting well without 'pigeon toes'.

The same swinging movement of the rod-tip can be caused by the incorrect use of the wrist, which results in curved line shapes when viewed from above. This problem can be overcome by imagining the rod-tip is casting beside a tall, long wall which leans away at 15 degrees. When you make positional checks, ensure that the rod-tip is moving beside this imaginary 'wall'. Now, you may be slim and have a 'good wrist', but do not assume that you are immune from twisting. Give the pigeon-toes-and-casting-along-the-wall technique a try. You may be surprised at the difference it makes.

As soon as you feel confident about putting a sequence of casts together almost instinctively, take your left hand out of its pocket. But make sure you keep your left hand beside the pocket and hold the line without letting it slip before you move to the next stage. This may take more practice than you think, because you will be concentrating on casting and forgetting about gripping.

RETRIEVING LINE

YOU'LL NEED TO draw line back after each experimental shoot, and the figure-of-eight retrieve is too slow a method to use. What do you do?

With the line extended on the grass in front, hold the rod in your right hand and position your upper arm vertically downwards and close to your side. Your lower right arm and your rod should be aligned and pointing directly down the line. Reach forward with your left hand and encircle the line below the bottom ring with your thumb and as many fingers as you choose. Then draw your hand back, letting the line slide through until it is just below your rod hand. You can now drop the index or middle finger (it's a matter of choice) of the rod hand, hook it around the line and then grip lightly.

With your left hand now just behind the index or middle finger of your rod hand, keep hold of the line, but release the right finger sufficiently to allow the line to slide smoothly through, and pull slowly sideways and downwards with the left hand. Stop after pulling, say, 2 feet and grip the line again with your right finger. Now release the line from your left hand and raise that hand to your rod-hand finger, grip the line below it with the left hand, release the rod-hand finger slightly, and pull again. In practical fishing, the length and speed of the left-hand pull and variations of movement imparted to the fly will be infinite, depending upon the type of fly being used and the mood of the fish.

SHOOTING LINE

THE ACT OF shooting line takes place as the line is extending during the forward cast and performs the vital function of increasing the fly-to-angler distance again. DT lines may be lengthened by up to five shoots, the first four in the air and the final one on to the water. WF and ST lines are sent to the desired fishing distance by one shoot only, after the head has been positioned outside the rod-tip.

The DT line is the basic line with which to learn to cast because of the slower, rhythmic feel of the casting strokes needed. No other line gives this 'feel', and it is a great mistake not to begin with it. Some anglers use WF and ST lines almost exclusively and find great difficulty in slowing down to cast a DT when conditions demand. Unfortunately, however, the DT line does not begin to shoot well until about 40 feet are in the air, a length which a beginner will be unable to keep up. So another method is needed if quick and continuous progress is to be made.

Shooting-heads provide a good basis for your first efforts at shooting line, so attach the appropriate reel to the rod and thread the 30-foot ST line and leader through the rings. Run the line out on the grass, leaving 2 feet of backing between the rod-tip and the ST. Now, holding the rod, pull out 6–7 feet more of braided nylon and, while maintaining the 2 feet outside the rod-tip, grip the line as before and put your hand in your pocket. Start a casting sequence exactly as you did with the DT line, but be prepared for a difference. Although the casting method is identical, your first impression will be that things are happening much more quickly. Try to slow down until you have a good line loop going backwards and forwards, which will be created by a flowing arm movement ending in a precise flick and stop. Most people develop ripples and a few sideways wriggles in the line at this stage, but these can be prevented by blending the arm acceleration with the flick and stop more smoothly and casting the rod-tip along the imaginary wall. By the way, make sure that the line does not 'click' in the tip ring or make more than a 3-foot overhang.

Have a rest after each sequence of five or six consecutive casts, because at this stage you will still be gripping too tightly and generally tensing your muscles too much. Try to relax and create a flowing style.

Once you feel in full control of the shooting-head, take your hand out of its pocket but keep it beside it and make a few casts while gripping the braided nylon between the thumb and forefinger. Now, how many times did you let the backing slip while thinking about the rod hand? Yes, I believe you! Keep working at it. Once casting has become instinctive, you'll be able to think more about that left hand gripping the line.

The method of shooting line is probably subject to more misunderstanding than any other aspect of casting. Pull out 12–15 feet of additional backing from the reel and drop it on the grass. Now, make a normal forward cast without extra effort, but this time open your grip on the backing when the line loop is about two-thirds extended. The backing will literally shoot up the rod rings and the line will straighten much further out before falling on the grass.

The stimulus for the release is entirely visual, so watch the line carefully and, during a practice casting sequence, say 'Now!' to yourself several times at the release point. Then do it 'for real' and shoot line. If you cast well, you will need some extra backing, so pull more from the reel – but no more than the pull of the line tightens to the reel at the end of each shooting cast.

You will realise after a while that your line release has become instinctive, though it may vary slightly with different lines and in different weather conditions. But as a rule the one-third:two-thirds ratio will suffice.

But two main problems may develop. First, most people release too early – I hardly ever see a beginner release too late! Second, few

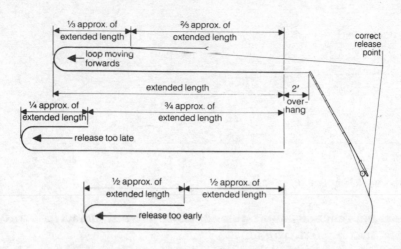

FIGURE 47: *Backing release point*

casters seem able to resist using too much force on the final delivery, with the consequent loss of speed and distance. This cast must be crisp, producing a fast, narrow loop. Keep the power output steady and extra distance will be achieved as though by magic!

Remember our previous practice casting: level/level; high back/low forward; and high forward/low back. Try releasing after casting in each way and you should find that a level back-cast followed by a slightly rising forward cast will produce the best distance.

The final point about basic shooting is that you must get the rod into a position that gives maximum freedom for the backing to slide through the rod rings. You can achieve this by dropping the rod-tip in the direction in which the line is travelling. Lower the rod-tip smoothly after the release is made, but not too much – between 20 and 30 degrees to the ground is correct. It is important, too, that you keep your rod hand extended in front and at shoulder height until the shoot has finished.

I have deliberately left until last my description of rod position as I do not want this final rod movement to be thought of as part of the casting action; neither do I wish to encourage those experienced fishermen who cannot resist putting great effort into the final delivery with a simultaneous lowering of the rod. All this achieves is a reduction in line speed which pushes the bottom of the loop

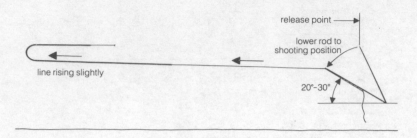

FIGURE 48: *Rod in shooting position*

down and generally spoils distance potential. It is, in fact, a formula for frustration and fatigue.

I've often noticed, too, especially among self-taught casters, a tendency to lower the rod hand to waist level and pull it back to the retrieving position after the final forward cast and while the shoot is still under way. Of course, the associated drag on the line, in the opposite direction, tends to shorten the cast, particularly when a DT line is used.

A recent example of this problem occurred when a friend with 30 years' river fishing experience took up stillwater trout fishing and came to me for help. He was not a bad caster, except for his habit of spoiling his cast as I have described. A bad habit practised for a long time is difficult to eradicate, and in this case a certain amount of social strain developed. Drastic measures were called for.

I asked him to cast between two bean canes pushed in the ground about 5 feet apart with a piece of wool tied between them at chest level. He stood with his chest about one foot behind the wool and cast over it. Every time he dropped his arm and pulled back, the reel hooked the wool. He eventually found it easier to break the habit rather than the wool!

Having become proficient with a 30-foot ST line, loop on another 3 feet of line between the shooting-head and braided backing. Now try shooting line again, remembering to wait longer for the line to straighten. Once you've mastered this extra line, you'll be able to add a further 3 feet, though a lot of practice may be needed before you can safely add the final length.

However, that doesn't stop you going fishing in the meantime, and the joined-up head can be used for fishing provided you don't mind the slight 'clicks' caused by the loops in the rod rings. When you can control the 39-foot length effectively, take the other half of the line out of store and make a one-piece head at a length to suit the fishing conditions you normally encounter. But a few words of warning: under no circumstances add length to the ST which causes you to spoil your casting style. If you do, your distance will suffer and you will expend extra energy unnecessarily.

It is now time to try shooting something a little more difficult – a WF line. The WF is simply a shooting-head with 'built-in' backing and is cast in exactly the same way, but the backing does not slide so freely. Ideally, you should start casting a WF with a head-length of 33 feet with 3 feet of the back taper within the rod rings. The best way to judge this is by painting a marker ring on the line (*as described on page 56*). The preparation for shooting this line is similar to that for the ST, except that you do not need to pull as much shooting-line from the reel. With practice, and using a good technique, you should soon be shooting more than 20 feet.

Having gained experience of shooting line, it is now time to stop laying the rod down and pulling line out on the grass before you start to cast. Using the WF line, hold the wool fly in your left hand, reaching across your body and positioned just to the right of the rod with about 12 feet of line (leader extra) hanging from the tip ring. With about 20 feet of additional slack between the reel and the bottom ring laid on the grass, grip the line coming from the bottom ring with your right index or middle finger. Now, make a gentle back-cast and, as the line starts to pull, release the wool fly. Let the back-cast straighten, then make a forward cast and let the line fall on the grass. Release the right finger grip and hold the same place in your left-hand thumb and forefinger. Make another back-cast and forward cast, shooting some line on to the grass, and stop.

You should repeat this procedure several times until you have extended enough line for a proper cast. As the line is lengthened, so it becomes easier to shoot, because the increased weight makes the rod 'work' efficiently. However, you must never use this system for fishing. The water disturbance would frighten the fish. It is worth remembering, too, that you should never whip a carbon rod quickly backwards and forwards with a short line. The internal stresses produced can damage some models.

Shooting the DT line must not be neglected, so change reels and run one through the rod rings. Extend 30–34 feet as described and have about 12 feet of slack ready to be shot. Prepare yourself for a slower timing, aerialise the line and, with a well-blended and accentuated forward flick and stop, release the line when the same two-thirds of the loop has extended. After a few experimental casts you will find the slack line shooting briskly through the rod rings. But do not expect too much too soon. Be satisfied with a short shoot if your casting seems tidy and under control.

You must expect the two-steps-forwards-one-step-back situation to develop at any time, but it is never more likely than when shooting. Your mind is thinking about the line and release-hand relationship, but forgets about the casting hand. At the first sign of difficulty, go back to basic casting, without shooting, to stop bad habits developing.

The last thing to learn about shooting a DT line is the method used for lengthening line while you are fishing. This uses three or four intermediate shoots above the water and a final shoot on to the water. For the intermediate shoots, grip the line between the thumb and forefinger of your left hand and, after releasing it, allow it to run freely over the three other fingers which are hooked around it. As each shoot exhausts itself, grip the line again and start a back-cast without allowing the line to fall. On the last forward cast, open your left hand and allow the line to run free. Once you have gained control of lengths in excess of 38 feet in the air, the increased weight of line moving forwards will enable you to develop quite long shoots. Don't try to progress too quickly at any stage, and should you find extra force creeping into your casting, realise that you are trying to compensate for the lack of a long, smooth acceleration and final rod-recoil speed.

Chopping down with the rod on the last forward cast is a common fault which is caused by the caster thinking that a large amount of downward movement is needed to change the line position from that of a level false cast to just above the water. The theoretical downward movement is quite small (*see page 22*), and the subtle changes may be difficult to grasp in practice, so I recommend a simple training system.

- Start a sequence of level casts with 30 feet of line and stop.
- While maintaining a level back-cast throughout, cast one level forward cast and thereafter lower the leader end one foot on each successive forward cast until it touches the grass.
- Without stopping, reverse the process until the line is level again. Then stop.
- Repeat the first three stages in 2-foot and then in 3-foot increments.
- Finally, cast level, touch the grass, and return to level again. Then stop.

You will be surprised at the small changes needed in hand movement to make quite large changes in the height of the line.

The last point to consider about casting a DT line is the position of the rod while the shoot is being made. It should be controlled by two factors: the need to prevent the heavy line-belly being pushed significantly downwards; and the need for the upward angle of the rod to be such that the heavy line will slide freely. The solution is a compromise, with the best rod position for the intermediate casts being at 20–30 degrees to the horizontal, and for final cast at 10–15 degrees. The lowering of the rod during the intermediate forward casts can be used as the forward cast 'drift' (*see page 70*), provided it is performed with care and precision after the rod has recoiled.

——— *DISTANCE-CASTING WITH* ——— *THE DOUBLE-HAUL*

I USE THE WORD 'technique' to imply considerable skill in movement, and in double-hauling the skill is in the dynamic use of the left hand while casting with the right in a conventional way. Double-hauling requires the caster to pull quickly downwards with the left hand in harmony with every casting stroke of the rod. Seen for the first time, it is difficult to imagine how this apparently conflicting movement can help, but it does, and in a dramatic way. Once mastered, the double-haul can be used with any line and will greatly increase casting distance and help reduce fatigue.

The technique is best demonstrated here in a series of drawings (*Figures 49–54*).

In theory, the downward pull should accelerate at the same rate as the rod, and the upward movement should decelerate at the same rate as the line extends and comes to a halt in the air. In practice, at least to start with, a quick pull down and a gentler upward movement will suffice. The longer the length of line outside the rod-tip, the longer each haul should be, which is demonstrated when you see a really good caster aerialising 60 feet of DT line when his 3-foot haul appears to be in slow motion. It is sad, but one often sees anglers hauling like fury, apparently hell-bent on dislocating a shoulder. This is totally unnecessary. Equally, the lovely, smooth, crisp action of an excellent shooting-head caster dispatching 38 feet of line to more than 40 yards with a haul of only 2½ feet is a joy to behold.

So, how does double-hauling help the fly-fisher? The benefits are more than might be supposed.

First, the **downward haul** helps to remove any ripples in the line and starts the line moving in the air instead of leaving it all to the rod hand. Then, because there is an equal and opposite reaction to the pull of the left hand, the line, in effect, becomes heavier. This, in turn, causes much more rod flexure for the same amount of rod-hand movement, which is transformed into increased casting energy.

Second, the **upstroke**, or 'rise up' as I call it, brings the line gently to 'rest' in the air, giving a much smoother line action. If it were not used, particularly with ST and WF lines, there would be an abrupt halt as the loop straightened and the line pulled against the rod-tip. This would cause a shiver, or ripple, in the line which would have to be straightened by the rod, thus wasting movement that should be accelerating the line.

Before trying to double-haul, study the drawings, make casts with an imaginary rod, and practise hauling in the correct sequence. Keep doing this until you can complete a sequence with

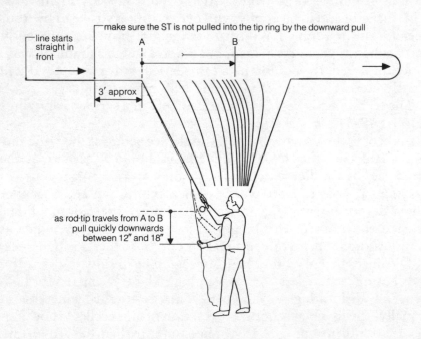

FIGURE 49: *Back-cast – part 1 for all lines, ST shown*

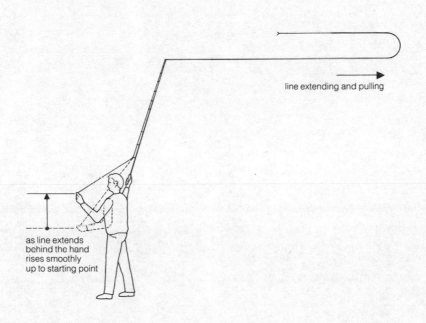

line extending and pulling

as line extends behind the hand rises smoothly up to starting point

FIGURE 50: *Back-cast – part 2 for all lines, ST shown*

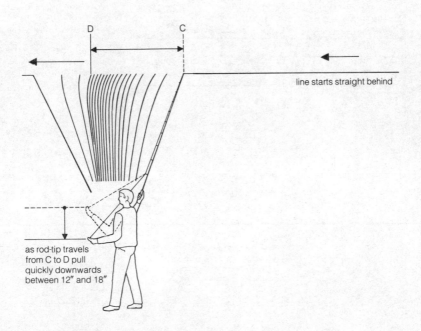

line starts straight behind

as rod-tip travels from C to D pull quickly downwards between 12″ and 18″

FIGURE 51: *Forward cast – part 3 for all lines, ST shown*

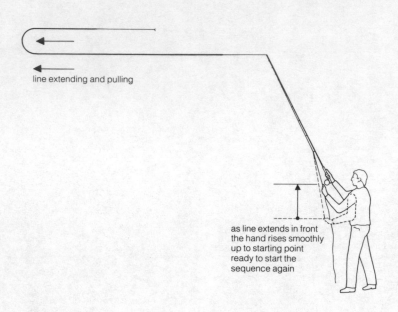

line extending and pulling

as line extends in front
the hand rises smoothly
up to starting point
ready to start the
sequence again

FIGURE 52: *Forward cast – part 4 no shoot for all lines, ST shown*

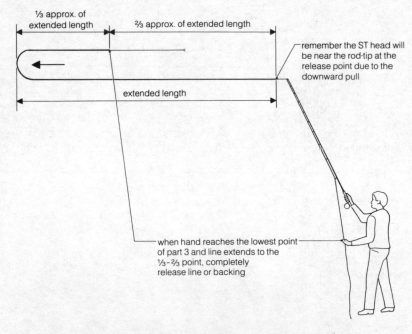

⅓ approx. of
extended length

⅔ approx. of extended length

remember the ST head will
be near the rod-tip at the
release point due to the
downward pull

extended length

when hand reaches the lowest point
of part 3 and line extends to the
⅓-⅔ point, completely
release line or backing

FIGURE 53: *Forward cast – part 4 the shoot for all lines, ST shown*

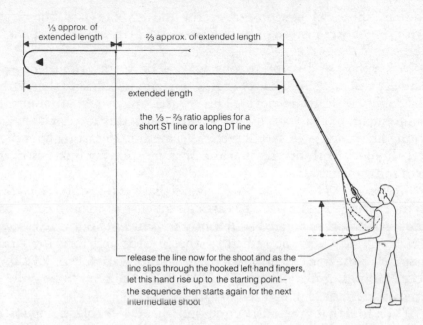

⅓ approx. of extended length

⅔ approx. of extended length

extended length

the ⅓ – ⅔ ratio applies for a short ST line or a long DT line

release the line now for the shoot and as the line slips through the hooked left hand fingers, let this hand rise up to the starting point – the sequence then starts again for the next intermediate shoot

FIGURE 54: *Forward cast – part 4 the release for the intermediate shoots with DT lines*

your eyes shut. As you haul, say 'Pull!' (because it is a quick word), and as your hand moves up, say 'Rise up!' (because it takes longer to say). Try to create a gentle rhythm.

You'll probably be thinking that there's no easy path to success with this particular technique; this isn't so. The problem for most casters is that their back-cast is not good enough to pull 2–3 feet of line or ST backing up the rod rings as the line is straightening. Solve this problem and you will be able to double-haul, since the forward cast is invariably good enough.

The quickest way to learn to double-haul is with a 30-foot shooting-head, which you can now easily control. Don't be put off if you have only a WF or DT line. These can be used, but learning may take a little longer.

Take up a normal casting position across the wind, having the usual 2–foot overhang and 8–10 feet of backing available for shooting. Aerialise the line, then cast and shoot *backwards* on a level plane, letting the line fall on the grass. All that really matters is that you should achieve a backward shoot as the line extends. Keep trying and you will find that you can make quite long shoots, though you may first have to endure many abortive efforts. Use exactly the same rod action and release point as you would for a forward shoot. Most people throw the line down towards the grass with some force instead of casting on a level plane with a crisp flick and stop.

When the wind is the 'wrong way' – on to my right side – I actually cast and shoot backwards when I am fishing and then turn the right way to retrieve. This causes a certain amount of amusement, but I always feel safer when doing this and can manage a long line when necessary. I prefer this method to casting over my left shoulder with my right arm across my body which restricts arm movement.

Increase the ST overhang to 3 feet, so that the line doesn't 'click' in the tip ring, and now start a casting sequence with both forward and back-casts accelerated sufficiently to cause a shoot if released. Then pull down as the rod travels backwards and forwards and 'rise up' as the line extends backwards and forwards. Provided the acceleration is good enough, your left hand will tend to be pulled up if it does not 'rise up' voluntarily.

If you find that previously good right-hand control is being lost, stop hauling, correct the rod control, and then try the haul again. You will probably have to do this many times before good co-ordination is achieved. It is like learning to ride a bicycle: one minute you can't, next minute you can – and you never forget.

Once you can produce a fluent sequence of casts with the double-haul, it is time to try shooting line. This is achieved by hauling down on the last forward cast as usual and releasing the line completely when the left hand is at the bottom of the haul and the line loop is two-thirds extended.

As your style improves, and the haul becomes instinctive, add 3-foot lengths to the ST in stages. You should find that your casting distance improves with each increase, particularly if the final delivery is precise and a little higher than the horizontal.

Next you should try double-hauling with the WF line. Your casting distance will probably not be so good as with the ST, because of the extra friction caused by the plastic-covered line in the rod rings. For the same reason, you may not feel so many of the subtle changes of tension in the line. The positioning of the down-taper in the tip-ring is important, so use the paint-ring 'trick' suggested on page 56.

You should find that the greater the length of DT line you can aerialise, the better your efforts at double-hauling will be. Once 38 feet or more can be cast with confidence and style, you will find the line loop produces sufficient pull to lift the line through the rod

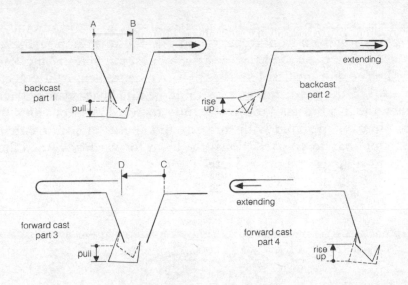

FIGURE 55: *Abbreviated double-haul sequence of false casts*

rings. Friction will eliminate most 'messages' from the line, so your double-haul movements will have to be instinctive. To shoot DT line while you are making intermediate casts, you should release line at the bottom of the haul and allow it to slide through the hooked fingers of the left hand as it lifts. Then grip it at the top and pull it down again to make the next back-cast. Fully release the line on the last forward cast.

By all means practise different angles of forward cast while keeping the back-cast level or slightly higher. But haul well and make the line really fizz out with three good shoots as if into the wind. The closer to the grass you can put the line during the forward cast without it actually touching, the further you will cast into a wind, since the line will not be blown back much as it eventually falls. Remember that when the DT back-cast is above the horizontal, falling energy can be converted into forward energy. If it is low, energy may have to be wasted in lifting it up.

LINE-LOOP SIZES

MANY FISHING situations demand a long cast, but this can be achieved only with a narrow line loop of, say, 2–4 feet, which minimises air-resistance. So it is useful fully to understand how to control the size of a loop. It is greatly affected by the amount of rod-rotation from front to back, and good results can be achieved by accelerating the rod hand over the longest possible distance on a level plane. For the first 18 inches of movement, or more if you can manage it, the rod-hand thumb should be tilted backwards. Then, when the hand reaches the nearly fully forward position, flick the rod-tip over the hand with forearm and slight wrist movement, and stop. Say to yourself: 'Push the hand forward first, then flick the rod-tip over it short and late.'

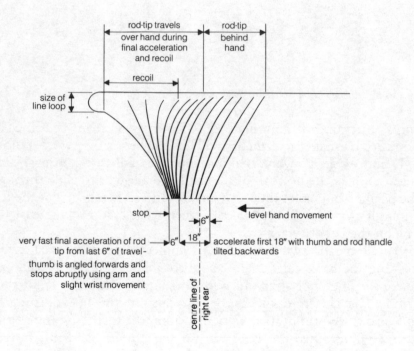

FIGURE 56: *The size of the line loop*

This level-hand movement usually produces a satisfactory loop which is controlled by the amount the rod-tip dips at the completion of the casting stroke. But don't under-estimate the amount of control needed, because most people chop downwards instinctively. For the longest tournament distance casts, the caster's hand is pushed upwards slightly at the end of the casting stroke to counteract the natural dipping of the rod-tip on recoil.

The author with:

A large expanding fishing bag as an alternative to the waistcoat pictured on the front cover

A lightweight folding carbon fibre landing net frame and handle with lanyard (see page 180). The lanyard is passed through the net frame and net bottom, then tied with a half-bow knot. When the lanyard end is pulled the net is ready for use. The folding facility is only used when stowing in a car boot

Olive green boots without line-catching side-straps

Landing net with lanyard removed and the pointed end pushed in the bottom. The long handle also makes the net very useful for netting trout while boat fishing

An extended hood worn over a cap

A waterproof fishing jacket (one that allows water vapour out)

Waterproof trousers cut-off above the knees

In this clothing the angler is kept dry and comfortable in all fishable conditions

(Photos: Tom Charlton)

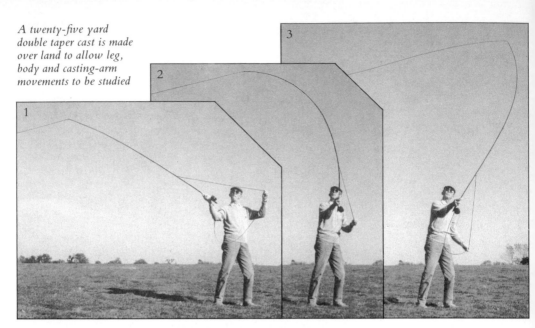

1. The line straightens
backwards. Rod hand
moves behind head and
rod-tip 'drifts' back.
Body leans back putting
weight on heels

2. Body and rod hand
move forwards with a
long, smooth
acceleration. The rod is
bent to the butt ring and
line starts to move

forwards. Wrist angle is
unchanged and rod
handle is vertical

3. Over the next three
inches the rod hand stops
and wrist angle closes
slightly. The rod now
starts to recoil and
straighten, pulling the
line forwards very
quickly. Note the
relaxed flowing
movement

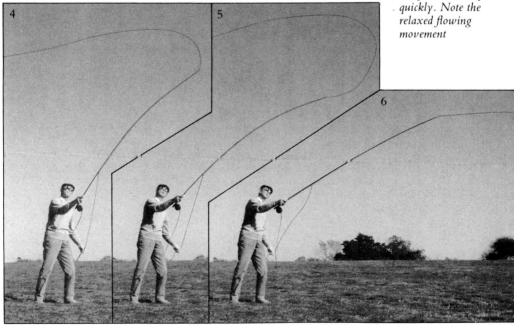

4. With the rod hand
stationary the rod recoils
to a forwards bend and
dips a little, causing a
loop to form

(Photos: Ken Lynch)

5. With the rod hand
still stationary full
forwards recoil takes
place. The very quickly
moving, rolling and

pulling line loop is fully
formed. Strong tension
at the rod-tip creates a
pronounced bend in the
line

6. The line is being pulled
forwards and the left-hand
release is taking place. The
rod-tip is lowered to provide
the best shooting position
and is now quite straight

Casting a shooting-head from a dam wall. A straight rod-hand movement finishes high at the back. The caster watches carefully as a tight casting loop forms clear of the wall and fence

Casting a double-taper line low into a strong wind, which will touch down at twenty yards in spite of a deceiving camera angle. Note: the body moving forward to add power to the cast. A narrow, penetrating loop forming. The final rod-hand position about six inches lower than usual

(Photos: Tom Charlton)

Trout food – Chironomid (midge) pupae and larvae (bloodworms). Note their lengths which are half an inch, or more

Weed growth – this angler has waded out to fish at the edge of a huge weed-bed

Trout food – coarse fish fry which provide a very nourishing diet. Note: none of the food items on this page have been damaged during ingestion

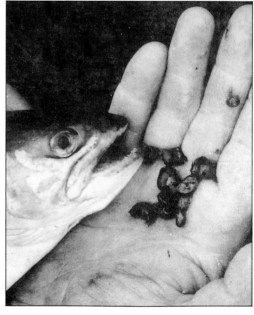
Trout food – snails, usually taken on or near the bottom, although very occasional floating snail migrations may be encountered

(Photos: Peter Gathercole)

The loop thus formed is extremely narrow, but it is made with a fly with the hook-point broken off at the bend which cannot catch up readily as might happen with a normal fly in fishing. On occasions, particularly when a three-fly leader is being used, the possibility of tangling can be reduced by casting a wider loop than usual, this keeping the flies away from the line and each other. This is achieved by the expedient of causing the rod-tip to dip further.

FLY PRESENTATION

ONE OF THE main reasons I have suggested that you should practise different heights and angles of forward cast is to ensure that you get the best possible presentation of the fly according to conditions. The best results will come with the DT line, but that is not to say you cannot optimise ST and WF presentations.

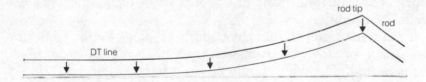

FIGURE 57: *Parachute cast*

You may like to try 'parachute casting' with your DT line. This involves shooting the line so that it straightens 3 – 4 feet above the grass, and then dropping your hand and rod-tip vertically so that the line falls gently. Try this at several different heights to prove that you have full control. The trick of getting the height right is to aim the thumb of your rod hand at the height at which you want the line to extend. With practice, you'll be able to 'parachute cast' more than 20 yards.

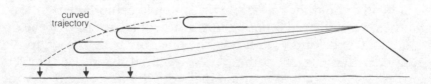

FIGURE 58: *Presentation, ST and WF lines*

Quite good presentations can be achieved also with ST and WF lines, but they are more difficult and 'parachuting' is not possible because the thin backing line does not fall in the same way as the head. Furthermore, these lines finish their 'flight' in a curved trajectory, so the height, velocity and consequent distance of the final delivery all have to be considered. You have to judge the right casting height needed for any particular line, so that all the forward motion is exhausted and straightening is complete just before it falls on to the water. It's not easy, but entirely practicable after some experience.

CASTING OVER WATER

IT'S AS WELL to have a little practice on water before you actually start fishing. A good idea is to continue with the wool tuft instead of a fly, and it is better if you can avoid trout water. It is asking too much of a serious angler to think about casting technique when fish are to be caught!

Ideally, the water should have gently sloping ground right into the surface, or a low, flat bank with grass and no obstructions for 30 yards behind. The wind should be from left to right.

The start

As you no longer have the opportunity to lay line out in front, you must use another method to put enough line beyond the rod-tip to enable you to cast. The problem is overcome by using a roll cast into the air, which is a modified version of the method described on page 90.

Having assembled rod, reel, line and leader, pull 30–40 feet of line off the reel and place it in your line-tray. Now pull about 20 feet of line through the tip-ring. Hold the wool 'fly' between the thumb and forefinger of your left hand with line from the bottom ring hooked and trapped under the other three finger-tips. Lift the right hand to hold the rod level with and just behind the right ear, and then, with the rod pointing upwards, tilt it back so that the tip is about 4 feet behind your head. The line now hangs down to the ground, with the leader coming up to your left hand. Pass the left hand across the body to position the wool 'fly' just to the right of the line of action of the rod hand.

To start a casting sequence, roll the rod-tip forward with a gentle acceleration and, as the line rolls forward and upward, release the wool when you feel a slight pull on the leader. The line will go forward and straighten reasonably well. While this is happening, transfer your grip on the line to the thumb and forefinger of your left hand, leaving the three fingers loosely hooked around it, and move your hand back to the left-hand side of your body. Once the forward cast is straight, make a back-cast which will put you in a position to start shooting line.

Line control

The first thing you must ensure is that you have developed sufficient line control to keep any non-fishing casts off the water. Many stillwater anglers extend their lines by casting on to the water, 'tearing off' into the back-cast, and then going forward on to the water again. With this happening three or four times before they reach a fishing distance, I'm surprised they ever catch a fish. They certainly spoil the fishing for those nearby.

In the easy casting environment we are considering you'll need only level backward and forward intermediate casts. Furthermore, with a WF or ST line, the level forward cast will suffice on the final delivery, because the curved trajectories of these lines cause them to straighten just above the water – assuming, that is, that your casts are not long.

Level intermediate casts are needed with a DT line, but the final delivery needs particular consideration. Clearly, it is not acceptable to have this 12–13 feet above the water, since it may be blown by wind or make a splashy presentation. Straightening should take place 2–3 feet above the water, and it is the movement of your rod hand that must cause this to happen. You can achieve it by taking your hand back in a level plane for the last back-cast and bringing it down at a slight angle on the final forward cast. Think back to your practice with the cane tilted downwards at the front and follow that example. You can experiment with different angles of tilt to achieve various presentations from hitting the water all the way up to the level cast, but you must keep your rod hand moving in a straight line with a brisk acceleration to straighten the line well.

Extra distance will materialise without any apparent extra effort on your part, provided you observe the 'one-yard-less rule' and have patience.

The lift-off

Most beginners retrieve their lines too far before re-casting. They therefore start with too short a line and find it a real fag to shoot enough to give the rod sufficient weight to work against. If you have this problem, try a roll cast into the air. All roll casting *must* be done on water, and initial practice is best done with a floating line. Retrieve line until 18–20 feet are extended on the water in front, with the rod pointing down the line. Now turn the rod 15–20 degrees to the right, lift the rod-tip and, while bringing your hand behind your head, tilt the rod-tip backwards 40–45 degrees in one smooth, steady movement. Keep the line moving back towards you on the water until it hangs from the rod-tip or, better still, moves slightly behind. Without stopping the line, roll the rod-tip forward and upward with a gentle acceleration and stop. The line will roll forward into the air and straighten, providing the basis for a normal back-cast.

This technique offers another advantage. A line being drawn

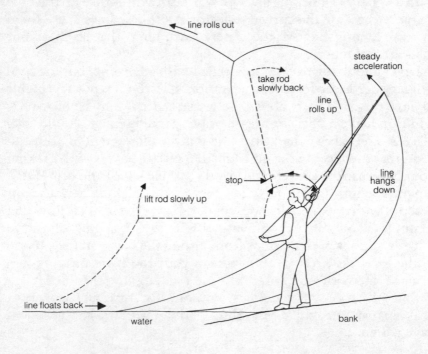

FIGURE 59: *Roll cast into the air*

back for a normal back-cast pulls the fly quickly through the water after a slower retrieve. A fish sometimes sees the fly make this darting movement from some distance away and decides to take. It swims fast to take the fly, and breaks the leader in the process! This often happens over deep water close in to a dam wall or in similar situations, but is less likely if a roll cast is used because the line is not taut.

Sinking lines can be 'rolled' out of the water in the same way, except that you may have to use two or even three 'rolls' when dealing with an extra-fast sinker.

Fishing Problems

THE DAM WALL

EARLY SEASON TROUT often feed in deep water, and trying to catch them may entail fishing from the dam wall, where they are within casting range. For the beginner, dealing with the high wall behind and the deep water almost beneath his feet is a real problem.

You know what to do, though. . . . Yes, tilt the arm action so that the rod hand travels up at the back and down at the front. If you've practised this thoroughly, you can change casting angles at will – hence my suggestion that you practise with the cane tilting down at the front.

WADING

MANY LAKES and reservoirs have shallow margins in which you have to wade to be able to reach a fish-holding depth of water. The deeper you wade, the closer your extending line is to the water in front and the bank behind. In this situation, you have to make the rod hand travel in a substantially level plane and then perform the 'flick' and stop at the end of the movement in a slightly upward direction at front and behind. This is usually more important on the back-cast, so that the fly is kept clear of the bank. However, it also helps in making the shooting cast with an ST line. To achieve maximum distance, your final delivery should be angled slightly upwards. Given care and persistence, you'll find that you can tilt the 'flick' and stop to some advantage while wading.

Another difficulty that arises for the wading fly-fisher concerns double-hauling, where the energetic performer can 'dunk' his left hand. So, if you double-haul while wading, haul slightly sideways, to the left.

——— *TREES AND BUSHES BEHIND* ———

THE BEST LINE to use when you've obstructions such as trees and bushes behind is the ST, because it needs a minimal back-cast and gives the maximum forward shoot. A WF line is a good substitute, but it does not shoot as far. If the obstructions are particularly close, cast at an angle to the bank.

——— *CASTING INTO THE WIND* ———

THE ONLY LINE that gives a worthwhile distance into a strong wind is the DT, and it should be cast as low over the water as possible, particularly on the final cast. The effect of the wind seems less close to the water, and the lower you can position the line and leader, the more they straighten. Presentation may be heavier than usual, but this has no detrimental effect on a rough surface.

——— *WIND FROM RIGHT TO LEFT* ———

THE BEST COURSE of action in a wind coming from your 'wrong' side is to turn round and cast backwards (*see also pages 83–4*). It's the supreme test of back-casting ability; and remember, the better your back-cast, the better your forward cast. It's an excellent way to improve your technique, even though your first efforts may be poor.

Safety

IT'S WISE to give some thought to safety before you so much as cast a fly. With the rod tilted away, as I have recommended, the hook is kept well away from you, but mistakes can be made, particularly if you are tired or cold, so *never* fly-fish without glasses of some sort.

Casting right-handed with the wind blowing from right to left, thus blowing the fly towards you, is a dangerous practice and is something I never do. If you really want to fish in this situation, cast over your left shoulder or turn round and cast backwards as I have already suggested.

Always take discarded leaders home and chop them into 3-inch lengths or less before disposal. Also, do your best to retrieve leaders hooked up in bushes or on fences. You may save a bird from a painful death.

The tops of dam walls are marvellously expensive places for losing flies. I once found ten flies in various states of disrepair over a 50-yard length, and it took me only five minutes. 'So what?' you may say. Well, how many times have you seen anglers kneeling down while attending to fish or tackle? A fly in the knee isn't much fun!

If you have to walk behind a fisherman, make sure you are safe from his back-casts. Never assume that he has seen you. He is more likely to be concentrating on his fishing.

If you are wading, particularly as water levels drop in supply reservoirs, large and small, watch out for soft spots and holes and old ditches in the bottom.

Dam walls can be very slippery when wet after the water level has dropped and great care is needed when fishing off them. If

94

you're careless, you may join the many other anglers who have been 'launched' down such a slipway – and remember, the water is usually deep off a dam wall.

... AND AFLOAT

ALWAYS TREAT boats with respect. It may become impossible to row back against a gale, so make your way back in good time if the wind starts to rise. Check that oars and rowlocks are in good shape before you go out. A broken or lost oar could spell disaster. *Never* stand up to cast. If your partner rocks the boat accidentally, you may actually cast yourself over the side. If you are a non-swimmer, wear a buoyancy vest at all times. Indeed, wear one even if you can swim, because the main danger in going over the side is that you may hit your head on the way.

An example of what can go wrong for the unwary even on the bank happened to me during my first season of trout fishing. It was a cold, blustery day and I was on a high bank at one of the Bristol reservoirs, casting a DT line and a small double-hooked Black Lure. Just as I had extended a long, somewhat laboured back-cast, the wind gusted from a slightly different direction. The result was that as I cast forward, the fly hooked into my coat between my shoulder-blades. My natural reaction was to reach up with my right hand to free the fly. I did, fumbled and hooked my thumb right over the barb. Just think about it – and about rowing home with a fly in a thumb if it happened in a boat!

Choosing a Fishery

Y OU MUST GIVE careful thought as to which water or waters you intend to fish if maximum enjoyment is your prime consideration. Fishing gives you a real chance 'to get away from it all', and the pleasure derived should not always be measured in numbers of fish caught. I would be less than honest not to admit that the catching of an occasional 'whopper', or a fine limit-bag, can be a real boost, but the essence of trout fishing is that while it is an active sport, we are concentrating on outwitting the fish, and it is this concentration which makes us forget less desirable matters.

The choice of stillwater fly-fishing is now vast, and it is impossible to specify what will suit an individual. It is a matter of taste, and forethought and planning are necessary to achieve the desired result. The best way is to try several different fisheries at the start of your career, on either a day-ticket or invitation basis. The most successful anglers are generally those who fish a particular water regularly, so although you are unlikely to catch large numbers of trout at first, at least you will be able to judge your improvement from experience.

When you do come to choose a single fishery on which to base your fishing, the most important factor may well be the time available in view of domestic and work commitments. You must make a careful assessment if best value for money is to be had. Few of us have unlimited cash, so it is logical to seek the optimum. As a guide, I suggest that if you have:

- One afternoon or one or two evenings per week for fishing, you should choose a fishery of up to 5 acres.
- One day and possibly one evening per week, up to 20 acres.
- Two days or more per week, more than 50 acres.

These suggestions are made on the basis that you will have a chance to get to know the water on the one hand and not be bored on the other.

You must understand the nature of a fishery and the facilities offered before taking your investigations further. The three main categories to choose from are the following:

—— SPECIALISED TROUT LAKES ——

THESE ARE MANAGED solely for trout fishing and are generally run by the proprietor or his bailiff. As they can function in the long term only, on the basis of customer satisfaction, considerable attention is usually paid to looking after the fishery. However, this is not always the case, particularly in respect of weed growth! Being lakes, their water level will remain relatively constant, but depth and the type of bottom will govern the amount of weed produced in a specific fishery. Deep water of 20 feet or more within casting distance of the bank can be a real advantage in summer because it remains clear. Shallow water produces large amounts of weed which, while helping to provide food, makes fishing difficult.

Many anglers view a lake early in the year and see only fishable water. In May the weed starts to grow around the sides at an alarming rate, and where previously a sinking line could be used to get down to the feeding fish, now only a floater can be employed. As the fish are still feeding deeply in the day-time, they cannot be caught so frequently, and often one has to rely on the evening rise for some sport. Then further weed growth in June and July is such that it is worth fishing only from boats – and the fishery may not have any! However, efficient chemicals are available to control weed growth, so it is important to find out whether this potential problem is dealt with efficiently.

— FARM WATER-SUPPLY RESERVOIRS —

LARGE NUMBERS OF small farm reservoirs have been created in recent years, and they generally provide a good environment for trout. Such waters are often rented by clubs or syndicates and stocked with trout. The normal arrangement is that the owner is permitted by the local Water Authority/Water plc to abstract water from a stream at times of high flow to fill the reservoir for use later.

The problems of water depth and weed growth are again relevant, except that the farmer may not be too thrilled about the idea of introducing chemicals or raking the reservoir walls!

However, the important factor to remember is that the water is a reservoir, and its contents will be needed eventually for irrigation. As the water level falls, so weed will become more evident and the bottom, usually clay, will be exposed. In times of drought, the water will be used ruthlessly and trout fishing will stop.

PUBLIC WATER-SUPPLY RESERVOIRS

RESERVOIRS BELONGING to water boards and companies come in all shapes, depths and physical construction, but they nearly all have one thing in common: a large acreage. They pose the same problem as do farm reservoirs in that the water level drops during the fishing season, but it does not usually do so as dramatically as with farm reservoirs, since a certain amount of water is pumped in during spring and summer when river conditions allow.

Their construction varies from gently sloping valleys with long reinforced earth dams through steeper, narrower valleys with short concrete dams, to complete concrete bowls. Dam walls usually slope steeply into deep water and remain relatively weed free, whereas the gently sloping 'natural' banks are subject to all the weed problems already mentioned. The most productive reservoirs, from the bank fisherman's point of view, are those with, say, half wall and half natural bank.

Another hazard, especially during August and September, is algal bloom. Vast quantities of bright green and blue particles rise to the surface and drift with the wind. The build-up on the downwind shore can be amazing and stretch for many yards out in a thick green layer, rendering large areas unfishable.

Most reservoirs have boats for hire and their use often leads to more fish being caught. Not only can more water be fished, but greater depth variations can be tried. Trout can be caught even on a baking summer day if deep water can be explored. Remember, though, that on many large reservoirs other water-sports are allowed – sailing and wind-surfing for example. With sensible rules and careful administration, problems seldom arise, but they do on occasion.

Any good fishery will have at least an adequate fishing hut, toilet, hand-washing facilities, scales for weighing fish and, most important of all, a bailiff or manager. Apart from being a useful source of information, he or she should be able to provide a detailed record of all fish caught. This is not only a useful guide to anglers, but provides the vital data needed by the management to maintain adequate trout stocks. One should be wary of fisheries where such records are not available. Some fisheries have superb facilities extending to rest rooms, bars and catering.

The most outrageous tale I ever heard about fishery organis-ation, or its lack, concerned a lake in Essex which is attached to a trout farm. During the afternoon the manager turned up with a net and proceeded to remove some fifty good-sized trout without comment. It transpired that the over-the-counter trout sales had boomed and more stock was needed. The anglers weren't pleased!

Catch-returns provide a good guide as to the quality of the fishing, particularly in regard to seasonal trends. However, they can also be misleading, especially if boat and bank catches are not categorised, because boats are more closely supervised than are bank anglers, who often make no return if they have a blank day. Not knowing the number of blanks can considerably distort the published rod-average. If this information is not obtainable, then you have to make your own assessment. However, my own experience is that the boats have the best of it, especially between 10 a.m. and 6 p.m.

Ultimately, your chances of success are controlled by the management's stocking policy. But never be deceived: the rearing of large stock-fish is subject to basic economics, and if you expect consistent catches of big fish, you must expect higher-than-average fees. Many fisheries disclose their stocking policies, which is a comfort to the angler; but one important aspect still to be considered concerns over-wintered fish which may be there to be caught in the following season. Sadly, as many as 95 per cent of rainbow trout and 50 per cent of brown trout die in some fisheries, so the residue from the previous season should be completely discounted where rainbows are concerned and a conservative view taken for the browns. There are many exceptions, but hard evidence should be produced if you are to be convinced.

Most trout fisheries have limits on the number of fish an angler may take in a given period. These are usually straightforward, but give some thought as to what will suit you. The most common limits for a day's catch are four, six or eight trout, so two or three good days in succession may present problems in preparing and storing the catch. But, please, do not sell them! If you have surplus fish, give them away, but don't turn your sport into a business. Some angling 'fishmongers' I have known reached the stage when they didn't know whether they were fishing for pleasure or the money. Some fisheries offer a half-day ticket with a reduced limit, which is useful if time is limited. Others specify a number of fish per week, or a low limit with any fish taken to be paid for at so much per pound. All these arrangements are acceptable, except perhaps the last. It is rather like buying trout 'over the counter'.

Another way of assessing the prospects of catching reasonable numbers of trout through the fishing day and season, as opposed to sporadic bursts of activity, is from the answer to the question: 'Do trout put on weight in the fishery?' Trout are great conservers of energy once they are acclimatised to a water because their long-term survival depends on it, so their instinct prevents them expending unnecessary energy by chasing after food. They wait until sufficient food is available for them to profit from the energy used in finding and taking it.

Fish freshly stocked from the stew-ponds are another matter. They have an initial burst of activity and take speculatively for a time as a result of their feeding habits developed while being pellet-fed in the hatchery. However, the survivors soon adapt to their new surroundings and, after a few weeks, begin to feed on the natural food available. This may be quite poor in some fisheries and an average-sized fish of, say, 1 lb may only just maintain its body weight, whereas a large stock-fish may actually lose weight. Quite long periods of inactivity may follow the initial flurry in waters with poor natural food supplies. They may last a day or two, or only a matter of hours. Longer spells are probably caused by cold weather keeping insect-life, which may be the main food available, inactive on the bottom. Shorter spells may end with the evening rise, when, as if a switch has been pressed, the surface starts to boil with fish taking hatching insects as fast as they can. This opportunist feeding is often pronounced in waters short of natural food.

Fertile waters do not suffer these stark contrasts. Trout are able to feed on the various food forms available over longer periods and thus provide much better opportunities for sport. When the weather is cold, fish will be feeding on snails and caddis on the bottom. When the water warms up a little, sufficient insects may become active near the bottom to encourage feeding, and then large quantities of daphnia may appear and the trout will cruise along sucking them in for hours on end. In large waters, it is this food that really makes the fish grow. The evening rise to hatching insects will also quickly be established in warm, settled conditions, and finally, large quantities of coarse fish fry may appear, providing excellent trout food. The effect of this continuing supply of food is that the 1 lb stock-fish of March becomes a fit two-pounder by the end of September.

All trout fisheries have their own rules, but they are basically similar. However, it is important to be aware of any restrictions – perhaps on hook sizes and shooting-heads, or on wading or drift-control rudders. It is a pleasure to visit almost any fishery, but do first make sure that the rules will not restrict your enjoyment.

Practical Fishing Through the Season

HAVING CONSIDERED the various factors distinguishing the different types of fishery, you should be able to make a fairly accurate assessment of which sort will suit you. So now is the time to give some thought as to how it should be fished, considering the time of year, and what you need is a series of easily remembered reference points outlining suitable equipment and flies and tactics that are likely to be successful. What follows, then, is a series of first-hand experiences in which something significant happened which is interesting enough to be worth passing on. They may give even the experienced angler food for thought, and possibly encouragement to try a different approach.

LATE MARCH: RESERVOIR BANK-FISHING

LONG EXPERIENCE of this water had taught me that good numbers of fish could be found in water 15–25 feet deep off the main dam wall. This extends for about three-quarters of a mile, with the best fishing usually adjacent to the deepest areas. In such a situation, it is comforting for the bank fisherman to know that he is likely to do as well as, or better than, the boat anglers at this time.

On the day in question the lightest of breezes was blowing along the wall from left to right as I faced the water. It was mild and overcast conditions, and realising that I would have a fair amount of casting to do through the day, I chose my 9-foot #8 rod as the least tiring to use with a reel holding 33 feet of #9 extra-fast-sinking shooting-head. My outfit was completed with a 9-foot long leader of 7-pound nylon, thoroughly degreased with washing powder and a drop of water, and a size 8 Black Chenille fly attached with a tucked half-blood knot. The reservoir was full, so I was well up the dam and could comfortably keep the shooting-head clear of the wall top and thus gain distance potential. It is unwise to use a long leader in such a situation because of the risk of it chafing on the wall top. A leader of less than 7 pounds is a poor proposition for the same reason. Since I anticipated a fair amount of walking, I kept my remaining tackle to an absolute minimum – a fishing bag and a landing-net with a lanyard. The breeze was not strong enough to blow the braided nylon backing about, so I left my line-tray behind to save weight.

Just as I was about to start walking, an early-bird friend arrived back with a six-fish limit, saying: 'All taken on a Viva from the second platform before the tower. Brian's on it now, and he's got two already!' (This dam wall has casting platforms at about 50-yard intervals, and the valve tower is at the deepest point.) By the time I reached him, Brian had caught another, so I decided to fish next to him. But though I expected some sport, nothing was forthcoming. Long and short casts, deep and shallow, fast and slow retrieves, all were tried – and with only one slight 'pull' to show for my efforts. Ian, fishing a similar distance on the other side of the platform, was experiencing the same as myself, while Brian caught his sixth fish. Ian then took over on the platform and caught three fish on an Ace of Spades. Meanwhile, after one and a half hours, I was still fishless. By this time I was really interested. Having experienced these 'hot-spots' many times before, I was half-tempted to stay put, just to see what happened. But eventually I decided it was time to find my own spot.

A 200-yard stretch on the other side of the tower was clear of anglers, so I headed for it, still wondering why so many trout should be caught from such a localised spot, and why they were there. Fifteen prime trout from an area perhaps 10 yards square? They must have been one on top of the other!

Having reached the clear length of wall, my plan was to start about 25 yards from the last angler and fish along the wall, ignoring the platforms. I achieved this by double-haul casting and then moving 2 yards to the left into the breeze while my line was sinking. It seemed a very long time, but was, in fact, about 45 seconds. I then retrieved the fly by pulling in one foot of line at a time, with each pull taking about a second, and allowing the backing to fall on the wall. After some 50 yards, I felt a good 'pull' from a fish which didn't connect. After another 20 yards without result, I began to think I might have missed a shoal, so it seemed appropriate to fish back again.

At about the same place I had a solid pull, followed by a sudden disappearance of the backing lying on the wall and then a scream from my reel. I was casting about 30 yards and the fish was hooked at 20 yards, but by the end of its first run, the trout must have been at least 50 yards away and still pulling hard. These early season trout may not jump much, but they run like fury!

Not wishing to lose the fish, which was obviously a good one, I played it on the reel so as not to risk the backing tangling and, after several dangerous moments, netted a beautiful rainbow of 3¼ pounds. Giving the fish a sharp rap with the priest, I inserted a long marrow spoon into its stomach, pushing the spoon in upside-down as far as possible, turning it the right way up and carefully withdrawing it. Nothing!

Slipping the fish into a plastic bag, and putting my fishing bag behind the wall top, I tried the same spot again, having checked that my leader and fly were in good condition. The very next cast produced another fish, 1¾ pounds, which contained four snails and three caddis larvae complete with their cases.

Having had two good fish, I re-knotted my fly for safety and made another expectant cast. Nothing happened. Thinking that casting repeatedly in the same place might disturb the fish, I cast at 2-yard intervals to the left. The third cast brought another solid take, and after a hard five-minute fight I had another good rainbow in the net.

A surprise was in store for me as I 'scooped' it. The spoon scraped on something hard on the way in, and it came out with three snails and two large stones – one nearly an inch long and the other 1½ inches. I'd seen plenty of small stones spooned from trout, but stones of these sizes were unusual.

The next half-hour produced nothing, and as the sun had come out, I thought a change to a size 8 Orange Chenille seemed a good idea. Orange flies do well in sunlight, and too often to be coincidence. Speculating that the fish might be higher in the water, or further out, I cast at a maximum range of about 33 yards and allowed 30 seconds' sinking time. In next to no time I had three more trout, two with no food and the other with three caddis larvae. These fish were all caught within about 6 yards on either side of the original successful spot.

I had chafed my leader once on the wall top and had replaced it, and I had once sharpened my hook-point on the small oil-stone I keep in my bag.

Having packed up, I sat on the wall to watch and think. Black flies have always done well for me in the early season, with orange or white as alternatives when conditions have changed or the fish have stopped responding. A shoal of trout sometimes seems to grow tired of the same fly.

Several anglers were on the move, walking long distances. Were they doing the right thing? They must have seen others catching fish, so why move long distances? A better proposition seems to be to locate a shoal of trout by moving a short distance, for it is quite clear that moves of only 10–15 yards can make the difference between no sport and good sport. As I walked back, I discovered that Ian still had only the three fish he had when I left him, so his shoal must have moved away, unless they'd all been caught.

This system of fishing, when trout aren't rising, has been my early season approach to waters of all sizes for a long time now. The only variation I make is in the sinking rate of the line in relation to the water depth. In very deep water a change to an extra-fast sinker saves a lot of time, even if you can cast only 18 yards.

My bag began to feel quite heavy as I walked back, and at the booking-out point I found that my catch weighed 11¾ pounds – without the stones, of course!

MID-APRIL: FARM RESERVOIR BANK-FISHING

THE TELEPHONE rang. It was Barry, who runs the fishing on a nice three-acre farm reservoir in Essex.

'Can you come over to fish on Saturday? They're difficult, but I think you'll enjoy it!'

Well, no one can refuse an invitation like that, so Saturday saw me at the fishery in calm conditions with cloud and some glimpses of the sun.

Barry was there with his usual cheery greeting: 'Must rush! Sudden business problem! Back in two hours! See what you make of it!'

The short walk up the valley to the reservoir brought back happy memories of the year before, and then, as I rounded the corner of the embankment at the shallow end, I saw the fishing hut, all spick and span with a new coat of olive-green paint. How good it all looked! But what a difference in the water conditions. Not only was the reservoir brim-full, instead of 6 feet down, but the water was gin-clear.

Now in counties such as Hampshire, this may be normal, but not in Essex! On my last visit the water had been opaque, with a green tinge and a lot of weed showing in the shallows. Today, all was transparent, and every tiny patch of weed could be seen on the bottom. Small wonder the trout were 'difficult'! But one or two were moving in the shallows about 30 yards away. . . .

Experience of similar waters had taught that the best rods to use in such situations are a 9-foot #8 in rough conditions and a 9-foot #6 on calm days. Accurate casting is often of paramount importance, and longer rods tend to magnify any errors in hand movement. So the #6 was the obvious choice for delicacy of presentation with a bright green double-taper #6 floating line. The colour was chosen for its good visibility on the water and against a broken-sky reflection, which greatly helps in judging casting range. A good, long leader was needed to keep the line well away from the fish, so I knotted 16 feet of 6-pound nylon to the line loop.

A careful reconnaissance seemed appropriate, so carrying rod, bag and net, I walked slowly along the deepest side. I was soon aware that three shoals of rainbow trout up to about 4 pounds were lying in the deeper water. With care I was able to approach to within 15 yards of the nearest shoal of about thirty trout without disturbing them. They were almost static in about 10 feet of water, but occasionally a fish would move sideways or upwards. It all seemed very peaceful. A hand dipped gently in the water confirmed that it was pretty cold, and with a slight nip in the air, it seemed that insect activity would be limited to the bottom. I carefully backed away to consider tactics.

With the water so clear and still, it was obvious that a few casts through the shoal with a sinking line would quickly disturb the fish, so my choice of line had been a good one. Their movements suggested they were taking insect pupae, but there was no indication of what they might be. A fly with general pupae characteristics was therefore needed, so what better than a Pheasant Tail Nymph?

It would also have to sink a long way, so some weight was needed in the fly. I always keep some size 14 Cove's Pheasant Tails, lightly loaded with copper wire, for just such occasions, so I tied one on and thoroughly degreased the leader. Now for the 'crunch'. . . .

It was crucial to drop only the fly and part of the leader over the fish, so I made a few measuring casts to get about the right length, retrieving by 'figure-of-eighting', and approached within casting range. My first cast was deliberately short, to make sure the line did not frighten the fish. I retrieved slowly and made another cast 2 yards longer. Being a double-taper, the line straightened really well and the long leader reasonably so, allowing the fly to 'plop' in just over the shoal. Now, with the aid of polarising glasses, it was just a matter of watching the leader sink and looking for any change of pace or deviation. But what was going on? The leader had slowed, but the fly wasn't on the bottom! Damn! That was an offer! Although I hadn't noticed, a fish must have risen a little to intercept the fly. But now it was going down again all the way to the bottom. I retrieved quietly. Nothing. . . .

Next cast I watched the leader carefully at the point where it penetrated the surface. Sure enough, it slowed again, but this time I made no mistake. Making a gentle sideways strike while drawing in line with my left hand, I felt a solid resistance. Now I had to keep the trout away from the shoal, so I put on good side-strain and the fish forged away to the right. It resisted the pressure, now from behind, and kept going for another 30 yards while I made my way quietly along the bank. Once abreast of it, I applied more side-strain, and off it went again, even further from the shoal. I caught it up again and the battle proper began. It was a good fight and a good rainbow at 2½ pounds. Its stomach held several light-brown chironomid pupae, so my suspicions were confirmed. A rest seemed a good idea after all the commotion, so I spent a quiet ten minutes just watching my quarry.

My next cast produced no reaction, but the one after produced another slowing of the leader, with the same result: a rainbow of 2 pounds 2 ounces, again with chironomid pupae and two small pieces of weed in it. Following another rest and the re-knotting of the fly, my next cast produced a different reaction. The leader sank for more than half its length, then suddenly moved sharply downwards to the left and just kept going. No doubt about this one! A gentle tightening caused the trout to rush upwards, boil on the surface and generally disturb the other fish. There was nothing for it but to pull hard and move carefully away with a big bend in the rod. Luckily, after some anxious moments, the trout followed. It weighed 1¾ pounds and contained more pupae and a piece of stick about 1 inch long.

It was time to try for my last fish to make a limit. My second cast produced another 'slowing-down' offer with which I promptly connected. This fish meant business! It charged off towards the shallow end, completely drowning the line as it went, with me hoping fervently that it wouldn't jump. But all went well and the fish eventually rolled over and went into my waiting net. Only then did I realise that I had an audience. Barry had returned and was greatly pleased to see the fish caught, especially as it weighed more than 3 pounds, but when I told him it was the sixth, he wanted to know how they were caught, too.

I explained my method and pressed my rod into Barry's hand. The leader slowed on three successive casts, but he didn't spot it in time.

'Can't get the hang of this,' he said. 'I've heard of the induced take, but this is the deduced take!'

His next cast was uneventful, but his fifth slowed again and the fish was hooked. No one could have been more pleased than he was with that two-pounder, and he went on to catch another shortly afterwards.

'This is more like chalk-stream nymph fishing,' Barry said over lunch in the hut, 'and we've been flogging these fish with sinking lines for an hour at a time. I suppose they could see all the casting disturbance. They didn't seem particularly frightened, but they must have been completely put off by it all. Come to think of it, the same must happen when the water colours later on, but we can't see the fish.'

'Well,' I said, 'it needs only one properly presented cast to catch a feeding trout. Make sure the long leader straightens by positioning yourself with any breeze behind and braking your final shoot with the left hand. That'll keep the line away from the trout. Then, when the water colours, the fish can see well enough looking out, but we can't looking in. So on small waters, where the fish don't move about a lot, it's best to have a cast or two and then rest or move, rather than flog away in one spot.'

LATE MAY: RESERVOIR BANK-FISHING

IT WAS MOST noticeable during the first warm week of the year how well the plants were growing in the garden border, and many were my silent pleas that conditions would remain constant until the weekend. As luck had it, nothing changed, and my Saturday fishing day dawned warm, but cloudy with a light westerly breeze. I was at the waterside by 7.45 a.m., with plenty of good places to choose from. The spot I had in mind was a point between two bays where the bank sloped steeply and the water was 15 feet deep 40 yards out. The breeze was blowing at a slightly outward angle from left to right, into the main body of the reservoir.

With waders on, and carrying two rods and my net and bag, I completed the half-mile walk in quick time with a light stride. The breeze was producing an ideal ripple, and already one or two trout were rising quietly about 50 yards out. It was easy to choose the correct outfits, and they were assembled by hands unsteady with excitement!

The shoals of trout which were off the dam wall earlier break up and range the reservoir once the weather warms up, following the currents and feeding heartily on the ever-growing food supply. Had the weather remained cold, as it sometimes does in May, then I would have been in no hurry to forsake the dam wall, but today was different. The trout would be 'running up the wind', fairly near the surface under the cloudy sky and often well out, so casting distance would be important.

My first outfit comprised a 9½-foot #8 carbon rod, a bright green weight-forward #8 line with a 40-foot head and a 12-foot long leader with one 4-inch dropper, 3½ feet from the point. A size 10 long-shank Cove's Pheasant Tail on the point and a size 12 weighted Olive Midge Pupa on the dropper completed the set-up. While a 9½-foot rod is more tiring to use over long periods than one of 9 feet, and brings a small loss of precision, the extra length enables you to lift a longer line off the water into the back-cast. This is an advantage with a floating line.

The fish were unlikely to seize the fly at close range in the shallow water, and 40-foot WF head-length ensured good distance potential and would turn the leader over reasonably well, particularly in the slightly helpful breeze. The leader was constructed from 10½ feet of 7-pound nylon water-knotted to 4 feet of 6-pound nylon for the point. Knotted up, it still gave 9½ feet of 7-pound nylon, 4 inches of 7-pound dropper (achieved by leaving one of the knot ends long) and a 3½ foot point.

My second outfit was my usual 9-foot #8 carbon rod, a 38-foot #8 neutral-density (very-slow-sinking) shooting-head, a 9-foot leader of 7-pound nylon and a size 10 Black Tadpole.

Why the two outfits and the choice of flies? In large waters, where trout grow quickly, it's odds-on that the staple diet of the

7 lb. b/s   cut off   point

6 lb. b/s

dropper

FIGURE 60: *Water knot*

fish is daphnia and midge pupae. Both these food forms are found high in the water or even at the surface when the weather is overcast and warm, and the trout simply swim up to the surface current and 'vacuum up' the food as they go. However, these organisms sink progressively deeper if the sun comes out for any length of time, the trout dropping down with them to continue feeding. So it is important to anticipate events and be prepared to go deeper as and when necessary. The floating line can be cast across the ripple and allowed to swing round, with occasional tweaks, but the flies will never sink more than a foot or so down because of the speed of drift. So you need a sinking line to get down, but a fly fished slowly on it will pick up weed all the time. By using a small lure, which will be fished faster because of its larger size, you can retrieve quite quickly without spoiling the illusion but avoiding the weed.

Having buckled the line-tray around my waist and degreased the leader of the 9½-foot rod, I waded quietly out for 5–6 yards and pushed the end of the landing-net handle in the bottom, to my left. I made a 10-yard cast slightly to my left, directly across the breeze, and simply allowed line and leader to swing round until they were well to the right, before I retrieved in small jerks. I followed this with another cast 2 yards longer retrieved with a steady figure-of-eight retrieve, and then a cast 2 yards longer again retrieved in 1-foot pulls taking two seconds each, causing the weighted pupa to rise and sink. On the third pull I thought I felt a slight resistance, but nothing happened. On the fourth, another 2 yards longer followed by a short drift and another pulled retrieve, the second pull was resisted strongly and a gentle strike had a rainbow leaping three times quite close to me before it raced off into deeper water.

After a first-class scrap, the fish was eventually drawn into the shallows to be netted at the second attempt. While the trout appeared beaten on the first occasion, the sight of yours truly and the net were enough to frighten it into action again. But the second time was better, and the fish, which was on the Pheasant Tail, slid into the net while I kept the dropper high, away from the mesh.

Two points are illustrated here: never cast far out straight away, since you may frighten fish that are close in; and the less movement the trout sees during netting, the better. In fact, if you ever hook a big trout on light tackle, a desperate measure that may avoid a broken leader is to stir up the bottom mud with your feet before bringing the fish in. I have resorted to this only once, as it can spoil the fishing for a time, but it was a case of 'needs must when the devil drives'.

The fish weighed just over 2¾ pounds and was as pretty a rainbow as I had ever seen. Spooning it revealed dozens of daphnia, looking like little jelly balls, and several brown midge pupae up to half an inch long.

Wading out again, I noticed a trout rise about 50 yards to my right and then about 40 yards away. If it continued on that course it would come upwind within 20 yards of me, so I waded faster, almost with indecent haste, casting at the same time, and presented the flies across the trout's anticipated path. The first pull came after half a second; then a second started, but never finished! Off went the trout into the middle distance with the reel trying to shake itself off the rod. I landed the fish after a prolonged fight to find it was hooked on the dropper, which calls for particular care to be taken in netting. Make sure the fish is completely played out, draw it slowly to the net and get it in first time. The risk is that the point fly may catch in the net before the fish is safely in. This fish was 3 pounds-plus and had daphnia, more midge pupae and two small pieces of weed in its stomach.

Two more rainbows of more than 2 pounds each followed, both on the Pheasant Tail, and then, at 10.30 a.m., the sun came out for the first time. Thereafter the spells of sunshine became longer and all surface activity ceased. The breeze also became noticeably stronger, which caused the floating line to belly sideways and drag the flies too fast. A change of tactics was needed.

I changed rods, degreased the new leader and waded in again, gradually extending the shooting-head to its maximum range of about 35 yards and trying different depths and slow rates of retrieve, but without result. Next I decided to go for maximum range and allow the fly, a Tadpole, to sink for about 40 seconds before retrieving it with fast draws of one foot in half a second. Suddenly I was stopped by a solid 'thump', but it was only a small stock rainbow with no food in it. The same thing happened four casts later, but this time the fish bored down and kept pulling in short dogged tugs. I was not surprised when a stock brown trout finally slid into the net. It, too, had an empty stomach.

That completed my six-fish limit, so fishing had to stop. It was too early for lunch, so I sat down to relax after what had been very enjoyable sport. This time for reflection is valuable, and it can reveal some interesting factors which affect your sport. Whereas it had previously been important to find a 'taking place' by moving position, all was now changed to a situation in which fish would follow the surface current and come to the angler, provided he was correctly positioned. However, this happened only while the weather conditions brought the daphnia near the surface and encouraged midge pupae to hatch. Once the sun had come out for longer periods, they had sunk to lower levels, changing the whole scenario. The bank angler must also remember on days such as this that while surface currents follow the wind direction, sub-surface currents may be different, for a variety of reasons, and fish may not attack a fly fished on a sinking line from a predictable direction.

Wind strength and direction are absolute controls on what can be achieved with a floating line. A general side-on wind may strengthen to the point at which its effect on the line makes it impossible for small insect imitations to be fished slowly enough. Also, the only condition in which a small fly can be fished very slowly near the bottom is when it is fished on a very long leader and floating line with the wind directly behind.

When trout from an established population are feeding in the surface currents, you are likely to catch top-quality fish that are growing fast. Once you are forced, as a bank angler, to fish more deeply, you cannot guarantee that the fish will be heading, and feeding, towards your fly. Your offering will be taken at the whim of any trout that happens to be in the vicinity, and as often as not, if you are using a lure, it will be a stock-fish rather than a keen feeder. It must be said, however, that this applies mainly to the first half of the season, before the fry shoals appear.

EARLY JUNE:
SMALL LAKE BANK-FISHING

WHILE LARGE reservoirs may be awe-inspiring in their size and their fish exciting, smaller lakes are more intimate. They are not so large as to seem out of scale with the trout and trees and bushes, and they often have a tranquillity lacking in a big, windswept water. One well-kept lake which I have fished has an area of about four acres in a stretched oval shape, with a line of trees along each side. The banks are either grass right to the water's edge or sloping pea shingle, and the water has a maximum depth of 14 feet. Wading is advantageous in places, so as to keep the back-cast away from the trees and to overcome the shallow margins. Although quite expensive, the day-ticket for a four-fish limit seemed good value in view of the environment and the fact that stocking was at daily intervals with trout all over 2 pounds.

The cloud was already broken with bursts of sunshine when I arrived at 8.45 a.m., and it was clear that staying in bed too long had been a mistake. One or two fish were moving at the surface in a light ripple, but their activity seemed lazy and without serious feeding intent. The outfits I put up were those described in the last chapter, but fly selection demanded careful thought. The lake carries a good food supply, but the size and density of the fish means that they do not put on weight.

In growing order of importance to the angler, the main food items are snails, caddis larvae and bloodworms (on the bottom or in the weed); hatching midges, sedges and terrestrial insects (on the surface); and sedge and midge pupae (mid-water and near the surface). Importance to the fish may be a different matter in that they are free to forage among the weeds and on the bottom, but weeds make it impossible for the angler to fish deep-down.

The lake's acclimatised trout are feeding on midge pupae in the early mornings and midge and sedge pupae in the evenings at this time of year, given normal weather conditions. The warm middle part of the day is relatively unproductive, with any feeding fish staying deep. Newly stocked fish are a different proposition. They are used to being fed on a highly nutritious diet at regular intervals in the day, but they are now in a new environment in which the pampering has stopped. They settle down over a period of a few weeks and, if they are not caught, learn to feed naturally, but during that time they are prepared to sample all sorts of brightly coloured flies provided they have sufficient bulk.

With this in mind, my selection for the WF leader was a size 12 Olive Midge Pupa for the point (as an obvious imitation) and a size 14 Invicta for the dropper. The Invicta is to my mind a useful caricature of various aquatic insects in the hatching phase and terrestrial food items as well. For the ST line I chose a size 10 Fluorescent Yellow Tadpole on the basis that probably the fish hadn't seen one before! Alternatives which I keep in my fly-box for such situations are fluorescent pink and blue.

Resisting the temptation to wade and remain virtually static, I put on wellington boots (with a view to keeping mobile) and walked round to the bank providing a following wind, watching for signs of activity. It wasn't long before I saw a quiet rise, 30 yards out from a small shingle beach. After putting on my line-tray and degreasing my leader, I made a gentle 20-yard cast with my WF line, followed by a slow figure-of-eight (FOE) retrieve into the line-tray (pea shingle, grit, plastic line coverings and rod rings are not compatible). My next cast I lengthened to 25 yards and the third to a maximum range of 32 yards. I retrieved both very slowly, while watching the end of the bright-green line intently for any slight movement. Nothing happened.

After my next cast had settled, I took two long paces to the right and allowed the flies to sink for 30 seconds before I made a fast FOE retrieve. Then I took another two paces, cast, let the flies sink for one minute and retrieved with a smooth hand pull of 2 feet in three seconds, *Pause, pull, pause, pull, pause. . . .* At the third pull I noticed a tiny movement at the end of the line, so I continued pulling and then struck – only to feel a slight resistance and then nothing.

This often happens with a pulled retrieve, because a fish has taken the fly gently during the pause and is already in the act of spitting it out as you pull again. Nevertheless, the pause-and-pull retrieve had indicated that a trout was interested in the fly being drawn upwards by the action of the leader and line. I took another two paces, cast, paused for 90 seconds (which seemed for ever), and then made a more or less continuous retrieve with 2-inch pulls. The line had moved no more than 3 yards when I felt a slight resistance and the line-end started to submerge. I responded promptly, only to be resisted by a tremendous pull and a huge swirl, followed by a half-airborne trout. Six eventful minutes later saw me slip the net under it, taking the usual precautions with a fish hooked on the point fly. It was a rainbow of just on 4½ pounds. Its stomach contained three bloodworms and five olive midge pupae, so the fish was obviously fully acclimatised.

Over the next hour I fished the full extent of the 30 yards of shingle twice more without an offer, in spite of the fact that fish were showing occasionally. This movement was surprising, as the sun had become quite hot. Perhaps they were stock-fish and a change of tactics would produce results. I cast my Yellow Tadpole to a full 35 yards time and again, moving with each cast in an effort not to overfish any one spot, but without so much as a tweak. Under the bright sun, things seemed pretty hopeless, so I decided to take a long break and, having made a final cast, started to wind in. I hadn't turned the reel ten times when a mighty pull was followed by the sight of a rainbow somersaulting and fin-walking. That fish weighed 2 pounds 10 ounces, but it had nothing in its stomach and I assumed it to be a stock-fish.

I was back at the lake at 6.30 p.m. with my thoughts on the evening rise. The little beach was unoccupied, and I put up exactly the same tackle as I had used earlier. Conditions were much improved, with the sun shielded by cloud, and a number of fish were rising as they had in the morning, but as it was too early for the evening rise proper, I retained the Yellow Tadpole because it was likely to provide the best chance of sport. I cast, allowed ten seconds for sinking, and retrieved steadily in 3-inch pulls. This kept the fly moving smoothly, due to the slight slackness in the line, and in less than an hour I'd caught two more rainbows of 2¼ pounds and 2¾ pounds. Neither had eaten anything, so it was almost certain these, too, were stock-fish 'just sampling'. So I still did not find out if an evening rise came.

A certain amount of self-discipline is needed after such a pleasant, almost casual day to stop, think it through and come to conclusions. It is all too easy to be lulled into mental inactivity by one's surroundings and success. However, the day had demonstrated two things: that once warm weather sets in from June onwards, the fishing day often breaks down into two good fishing periods – early morning and evening (I was too late in the morning for sport to be good!); and that not infrequently after a fishless period, a good offer will materialise as line is being *wound in* for a move or change of fly.

Even more remarkable is that this steady retrieve, as it is termed, is successful with small flies as well as large. This is often forgotten when the fishing is good, but when the 'going gets tough', it can pay to remember that some 'extra' fish may be caught in this way. Rather than winding in, the retrieve is accomplished by tucking the rod handle hard under the right armpit and pulling alternately with right and left hands over each other in a rotary motion, thus achieving the smooth fly movement needed. Don't worry too much about striking: all you need do is to twist sideways. If you find it difficult, think of a one-armed angler I knew who had to hold his rod in this way. His technique was deadly!

——— EARLY JUNE: ———
RESERVOIR BOAT-FISHING AT ANCHOR

WORD WAS THAT bank-fishing had been slow during the day for some time, so, having only a morning to spare, I decided to take a boat. The day was warm and overcast, with just the hint of a shower, and with a steady south-westerly breeze, ideal conditions, I thought, in which to find some rising fish, anchor up and generally take it easy. Drifting methods are less attractive when you are fishing single-handed because of the work involved and the time lost in rowing upwind again. I took only one rod, my 9-foot #8 carbon, but with a selection of lines in my bag. I put up my bright-green WF #8 floating line with its 40-foot head, knotting on a 14-foot 7-pound level leader with a 5-inch dropper 3 feet from the point. I chose the long leader because the water was deep and clear (which gave the fish every chance of seeing the line from below) and to keep the line-end away from any fish near the surface. Thinking that numbers of insects would be hatching, I tied a size 12 Allrounder to the point and a 14 Soldier Palmer to the dropper.

Having carefully selected a sound pair of oars, and a seat cushion, and loaded the boat (which was out of the water on a sloping bank) I made a few checks. Were the rowlocks secure in their mountings? Did the oars fit properly? Was the drain-plug tightened up? Was there a bailer and a distress flare? Was the anchor sound and its rope secured? Was the foot-rest firm? It may sound elementary, but a check takes only a minute or two and is worth every second, unless you wish literally to finish 'up the creek without a paddle'!

An example of what can go wrong concerned one of the same fleet of boats. Two anglers launched their boat and rowed off with keen anticipation. Having gone about 50 yards, they turned round and rowed back as if demented. They had every reason to hurry, because the boat was filling with water! I was hard put to conceal my amusement! The bailiff had apparently removed the drain-plug to let out overnight rainwater and had forgotten to replace it!

However, all was well with my boat, so I launched and rowed

quickly out to the middle of the reservoir, all the time watching for rises. Sure enough, lots of fish were rising with their noses just under the surface film, travelling in a general upwind direction. Eventually I anchored a few yards from a calm lane in which activity seemed most intense. Lanes such as this seem mysterious and can stretch for hundreds of yards. But they attract trout because insects become trapped in the increased surface tension of the calm water.

A boat must be anchored with care in such a situation, and I allowed mine to lie downwind with the rope over the bow. Most boats have minds of their own and never behave as one might expect, so I always carry a small G-clamp which I attach to the gunwale to effect minor adjustments to the rope attachment. To be safe, I tie a length of strong cord to the clamp and attach it to any convenient place on the boat. Mine has been over the side twice already!

I could see the trout swimming upwind past me, but with the boat lying downwind, few of them were frightened. It was comfortable too, be able to sit on the middle thwart facing backwards, as for rowing.

I covered at least ten fish in the first half-hour, but none of them showed the slightest interest. I varied my presentation and the flies were good patterns for the conditions, so obviously a radical change was necessary. The best course in such situations is often to try something dramatically different rather than to make minor alterations in fly selection. My ploy was to change to a #8 floating 36-foot ST with a 9-pound leader the same length as the first and to use a size 8 long-shank Grey Muddler Minnow on the point and a size 10 Grey Muddler Minnow on the dropper. More fish came through while I changed and I was obviously in a great hurry, but trying to take care at the same time. It is so easy to miss a rod ring or tie a knot badly if you are over-hasty.

I pulled 25 yards of braided nylon backing from the reel, and extended the ST. I hadn't long to wait. Another trout came within casting range, but it was in the most difficult position, directly downwind of the boat. In such a situation, casting length and direction have to be perfect if the fish is to see only the flies. Unfortunately, I overcast by a couple of yards and the trout saw the splash of the line and was gone. Then another fish came up the edge of the calm lane about 35 yards away. I cast at an angle so that leader and flies were across and beyond the fish's path and, when I judged the fish to be close, I began a retrieve of 2 feet per second. The flies, being nearly buoyant, produced two bulges in the surface film as they came across the trout's field of view, with immediate effect. The fish changed path slightly and began to snap at the point fly just like a dog after a rat. My hair seemed to stand on end as I made two or three left-hand pulls – and then the fly was seized in a huge swirl, followed by a tremendous pull.

The fish made a long run, slashing on the surface, and then sounded. Then back it came to go straight under the boat, leaving me thankful that it was moored at only one end. Some fish fight amazingly hard, and my 9-pound leader had proved very necessary. Five minutes later the fish was in the net, a nice 2¼-pounder.

Spooning the fish solved the problem of what the trout were feeding on, for it contained a mass of daphnia. Daphnia form a rich and attractive trout food, and the overcast conditions must have brought clouds of them almost to the surface, which explained the trout's feeding pattern. The problem is that once trout get a taste for daphnia they become preoccupied, and the angler has to give them a jolt to have any measure of success. My darting, highly visible Muddlers had probably aroused the trout in the first place, but the fact that one lure was apparently chasing the other doubtless had something to do with it as well.

Having found the right formula, I had no time to lose, for if the sun came out, down would go the daphnia – and the trout. Fish were still coming up the calm lane fairly regularly, and at times I could see them 100 yards away. Indeed, on three occasions I was able to cast to the same fish twice, having cast short at my first attempt. Sometimes they followed the flies right up to the boat, only to spot the danger and go down with a big swirl. Sometimes they boiled at the fly and then went on their way. Two more seized the dropper fly having visibly overtaken the point with an arrogance which said 'You're not going to have it!', and were duly boated.

At least two trout were put down when I cast over them by mistake, but the greatest interest was created by casting downwind and across the trout's path at between 10 and 20 degrees. This wasn't easy, because each fish, while heading generally upwind, followed a slightly erratic course, in either speed or direction. On three other occasions I was able to cast, wait, let the fish come to the flies, draw in slightly to get the flies in position, and then start pulling when the trout was inches away. The results were dramatic – heavy pulls and the fish hooked immediately!

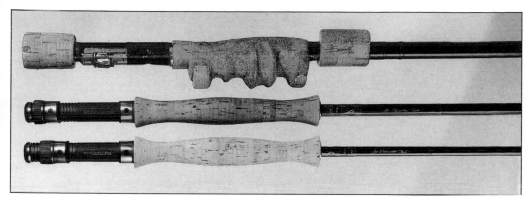

Casting distance – this is dictated by the power of the rod blank, assuming good casting technique. Top – the author's tournament rod has a butt diameter of 0.67 inches, regularly casting 60 yards. Centre – #9 distance fishing rod 0.45 inches, 45 yards. Lower – #8 general purpose rod 0.37 inches, 30 yards

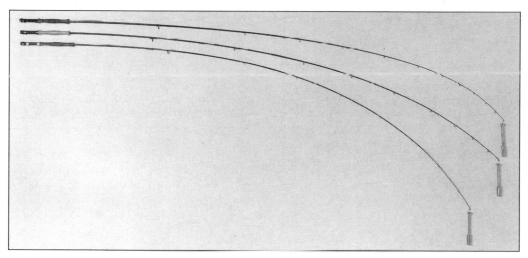

Rod action – these 9.5 feet rods, all rated #9 by their maker, are deflected by the same test weight (priests have other uses). Top – good tip action distance fishing rod, 22 inches deflection. Centre – good general purpose fishing rod, 26 inches. Lower – poor general purpose fishing rod, 34 inches

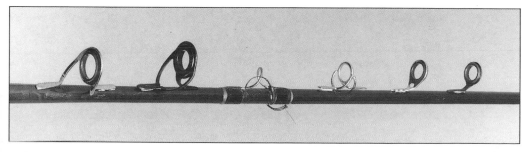

Rod rings – the whippings of the snake ring were sawn through by persistent double-hauling. The wire bridge ring is better but prone to grooving. Oxide lined rings are excellent, keeping the line off the rod and are extremely resistant to grooving

(Photos: Fidelity Studios)

3. *Rod hand rotates downwards, wrist angle closes and hand stops abruptly. Rod starts to recoil forwards and upwards. Line begins to lift from water. Rod handle angled forwards*

2. *Rod hand accelerates forwards and upwards. Large line loop forms behind. Rod bends against line weight and water friction (drag). Rod handle tilted backwards. Wrist angle unchanged*

6. *Rod hand lowered slightly. Wrist angle unchanged. Rod straightens. Line continues to roll forwards producing a large loop until the line is reasonably straight in the air, at rod-tip level*

Note: When used as a fishing cast the rod tip would start higher at the back and lower at the front, thus causing the line to straighten on the water

1. *Rod hand moves slowly back to a point opposite right ear. Rod angled backwards. Line floating and moving backwards, helping to form a large loop behind*

5. *Rod hand static. Wrist angle unchanged. Rod finishes recoil downwards. Forwards loop starts to form. Line leaves mark on water as it rolls upwards. Note: Rod-tip movement is nearly circular throughout the cast, and it is the long recoil while the rod hand is static that makes the cast effective*

4. *Rod hand static. Wrist angle unchanged. Rod continues to recoil and straighten while rod tip moves downwards*

(Photos: Ken Lynch)

What we all hope to catch – a perfectly conditioned double-figure rainbow trout   (Photo: Mick Toomer)

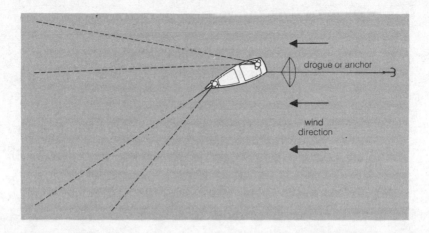

FIGURE 61: *Two anglers fishing safely at long range from an anchored or drifting boat*

With my sixth fish in the bag I had to stop fishing, and only then did I realise that I was wet with sweat. This had been the most exciting trout fishing ever – not purist trouting, perhaps, but very exciting!

CONCLUSIONS

SHOCK TACTICS often work when trout will not take well-presented and appropriate flies. Work fast when conditions are good and the trout are responding, because the weather can change quickly. Never use weak nylon when the fishing method is intended to incite the fish to take. Never be too proud to experiment if the going becomes difficult.

Since two anglers often share a boat, careful thought must be given to a safe casting system for DT lines or WF and ST lines with heads of 34 feet or longer. My experience is that it is *not* safe to cast long distances with these when a boat is moored broadside to the wind and one line is passing between two anglers, which is the case with two right-handers. A better idea is to attach the anchor rope, or drogue, near the corner of the stern (*see diagram above*) and to make the necessary adjustments. Two anglers can safely make long casts in this way, and if one position is more successful, then regular changes can be made. Safe casting in the broadside position can be achieved with up to 30 feet of DT line, or WF and ST lines having 30-foot heads. But the only truly safe method is to match a left-handed caster with a right-handed one.

MID-JUNE:
RESERVOIR BOAT-FISHING, LOCH-STYLE

MID-JUNE offers some of the best daytime opportunities for the boat-fisher. Good fly-hatches can be expected, and given a good ripple, broken cloud and short periods of sunshine, any rising fish are likely to be genuine insect-takers, since the daphnia will be deep down and fry shoals are unlikely to be around. Now is the time for the delicate art of imitating hatching insects and fishing in the most traditional of ways: loch-style. This presentation of flies is attractive to the fish and relatively undemanding for the fisherman, and because most fisheries large enough for drifting offer motor boats for hire, the effort of rowing back after a drift is eliminated.

The main need is a good breeze to drift the boat and to produce sufficient ripple to conceal the anglers from the fish at quite close range. To start a drift, the boat is turned broadside to the breeze and one or even two drogues are put in the water on the windward side. A drogue is rather like a square parachute with a small hole in the centre and four cords, one to each corner, attached to a large swivel at the end of a strong cord, about 4 yards long, which is connected to the boat. It slows the rate of drift sufficiently to prevent anglers having to draw their flies in too quickly after each cast. Drogues are available in sizes from 3–5 feet square, and having one of each means that any safe wind can be dealt with.

All boats have their individual drifting characteristics, particularly with two anglers and their tackle aboard, so each angler needs a 4-inch G-clamp which can be moved along the gunwale and used to facilitate the fine adjustment of the direction of drift. Some regular fishing partners go to the trouble of having an additional 2-foot square drogue made to maintain a precise downwind movement. Another aid to fishing comfort is a padded seat which rests across the gunwales with adjustable stops to prevent it slipping, but with only one of the two anglers using such a seat, the boat will drift at an angle.

Traditional loch-style fishing has one angler sitting in the bow and the other in the stern, each casting a maximum of 10 yards downwind, raising the rod-tip at various rates, back-casting and repeating the process. The longer the rod (10–11-foot rods are popular), the more the flies move in the water for the same arm movement. Keen anglers will have two rods of their chosen length, one rated #5 for light winds and another rated #7 for strong winds. This may seem to represent a high degree of specialisation, but there is no doubt that the #5 line is less conspicuous in light breezes and that the #7, being heavier, is less likely to be blown about in strong winds. However, most anglers probably compromise with a #6. With only short casts being made, it does not matter much if a 40-foot head WF or a DT line is used, except that some DT lines have a longer front taper, which gives a more delicate presentation. Leader lengths should be between 10 and 14 feet, depending on rod length, and have two droppers. The three flies used can imitate the rising pupa, a hatching fly and a hatched fly, particularly if the pupa imitation on the point carries some weight. The permutations are endless.

No fly-fisherman should fish without protective glasses, but loch-style fishing is the safest method of all. With a long rod held nearly vertical, a short line can be cast in a wide loop over the rod-tip, minimising the risk to each angler and tending to prevent leader tangles, even when casts are made at 15 degrees either side of the drift line.

Since my time for fishing is sadly limited, I have to make the most of every opportunity and often end up going out on my own, even when fishing loch-style. One such outing was on a fine mid-June morning, bright with patches of cloud and a good breeze – ideal, in fact, for a morning's drifting. Luckily a motor-boat was available, and this I promptly took.

I put up my 11-foot #6 carbon rod with a pale-green DT6F line and a 13½-foot 6-pound leader. Working from the point, I tied two 5½-inch droppers with water knots at 3½-foot intervals. My flies were: point, size 12 Mallard and Claret; first dropper, size 12 Soldier Palmer; second (or top) dropper, size 12 Black Zulu. Then I degreased the leader and flies, stowed all my gear, including 3-foot and 5-foot square drogues in the boat, made my usual safety checks, and set out for the far side of the reservoir, which was relatively clear of anchored boats.

Making two slight detours to avoid disturbing those already fishing (you should always pass behind boats, and then no nearer than 50 yards with the motor power reduced), I headed for a large bay which I knew from previous forays to be about 10 feet deep. Taking care to avoid the drift path, I turned the boat broadside to the breeze and cut the motor. With my G-clamp attached near the centre of the boat, I tied my 3-foot drogue cord to it and proceeded to drop the drogue carefully into the water. With the boat drifting two pulls on the drogue cord caused it to open out, so all was ready.

Unhooking my point fly from the keeper-ring, and pulling about 20 feet of line through the tip-ring into the boat, I flicked line on to the water and followed up with a lift, back-cast and forward cast proper. Then I brought the flies smoothly back by pulling and lifting with the rod while my left hand held the line some 18 inches from the rod handle.

This action caused the top dropper to produce a tiny wake on the surface, but feeling that the flies were working too close to the boat, I extended another 6 feet of line and then alternated smooth with slightly jerky movements of the rod-tip. As the boat drifted out of the bay over deeper water, so I tried different angles in front of the boat, but without response. Then up popped a trout 'from nowhere', splashing at the Zulu without taking and causing my heart to miss a beat.

My next cast was to the left and allowed to sink more. Then, with the line going slack, I lifted quite quickly and, just as the Soldier Palmer came to the surface, felt a strong pull as the fly was seized. A tough scrap ended with a 1½-pound rainbow in the boat. Spooning showed the trout had eaten a few small dark midge pupae, then I put it in a plastic bag and protected it from the sun.

I paused longer on my next cast to allow the point-fly to sink deeper, following up with a steady rod-tip lift speed of about one foot per second. However, this didn't work well because the boat was now drifting too fast. Replacing the small drogue with the 5-foot version slowed the boat considerably, and now I could allow quite a pause before lifting. Three casts later and the Zulu had just come to the surface when it disappeared again and the nylon started to tighten. My gentle, lifting strike caused absolute mayhem as a large rainbow jumped and swirled all round the boat, then suddenly gave up and came gently into the waiting net. It weighed just over 3 pounds and had daphnia in its stomach. The next 200 yards of drift produced only one abortive tweak, so I decided to try the same drift again after motoring round in a large semi-circle to avoid disturbing the fish. This time my point fly was taken firmly after only 50 yards, having been drawn quite quickly to the surface from the right. This was a smaller fish of 1¼ pounds with nothing in its stomach. With my short line and medium leader length, I could see all these fish taking within 10 yards of the boat – exciting stuff!

Casting is so easy as one sits in a drifting boat with the breeze directly behind – just a lift, a slight rotation of the arm to open the loop, an upward flick at the back, then a pause and slightly downward rotation with a forward flick. Hardly any physical effort is involved, but it's all very absorbing for all that.

After a further 50 yards another trout rose to the Zulu, but didn't take. I stopped for a moment in disappointment, only to be jolted into action almost immediately, since the fish must have taken the point fly as it sank – another rainbow of about 1¼ pounds with only a few olive midge pupae in its stomach.

To continue the drift over deep water was fruitless, and time was getting short, so I took another semi-circular return journey to start a drift 30 yards across the wind to the right from the previous one. Nothing happened for quite a long time, but then, just as the bottom of the bay started to shelve off, and I was about to lift the point fly off into the back-cast, there was an explosion of water as a fish seized it. But for the long, soft-actioned rod, the leader would surely have broken. A lot of high-speed surface activity followed until another rainbow of around 1¾ pounds came into the boat. Again, the stomach was empty.

Now it really was time to finish, so I laid the rod on the thwarts, lifted the drogue, spilling the water over the side, then started the motor. Motoring back to the moorings, I had time to reflect on an unhurried and relaxing morning which had yet brought good fishing. Hardly a fish had shown on the surface other than those coming to my flies, so they must have been attracted from various depths. But the most important factor had been to slow the drift speed and let the flies sink before being drawn back. Furthermore, fly movement had been made smoothly, by lifting the rod-tip instead of relying on left-hand pulling.

A wide variety of minor variations of fly movement can be successful. One is to use the wind to billow the line out while the rod-tip is moved sideways. This brings the flies across the front of the boat in the surface film, which seems attractive to trout at times. There is much scope for experiment with different teams of flies presented in a variety of ways, with drift speed controlled by the size of the drogue in relation to wind speed. A larger drogue slows the boat more, creating a greater billowing effect on the line.

Finally, and probably most importantly, the successful drift had been tried several times. I was lucky to find it in the first place and it pays to back winners! Some fisheries provide maps showing water depth, and these are useful when selecting drifts, particularly if the water is new to you. I like to drift over water 8–15 feet deep, provided the weather is not too hot. There is always the likelihood of a deep-lying trout being interested enough to come up to take.

Drift-fishing can be extremely effective during the evening rise, provided the breeze is enough to move the boat. Should the breeze fail, one of a pair of anglers can row the boat slowly and quietly, while the other fishes.

MID-JULY: RESERVOIR DEEP-DRIFTING

DAYTIME FISHING can be difficult at most trout fisheries when the weather is warm in July and August. Bank-fishermen may find the early-morning rise quite good, and the evening rise prolific in terms of fish seen, but not necessarily caught. Boat-fishing is not usually allowed until eight or nine o'clock, so boat-fishers are left with the prospect of fishing through a possibly unproductive day or waiting for the evening rise. But some fisheries offer afternoon or evening boat tickets, so if boat-fishing is your choice, you may well have excellent evening sport by fishing loch-style as already described.

However, I am concerned here mainly with those who do wish to fish through the day, from say 9 a.m. to 6 p.m., for whatever reason. The method of fishing I am going to describe is used throughout the season, but in July, August and September it probably helps the boat-fisher to catch more than his counterpart on the bank.

Acclimatised fish will be growing rapidly in large fertile waters, while shoals of recently stocked fish will still be getting used to their new environment. So it really is a question of locating groups of fish and presenting attractive offerings. In July the natural food supply is large and varied even during the day: midge and sedge (caddis) larvae, snails and shrimps, midge and sedge pupae preparing to hatch, water boatmen, 'clouds' of daphnia (though these may stay deep if overhead conditions are bright), and often large shoals of coarse-fish fry. But not much activity will be apparent at the surface, so it is a matter of searching as much water as possible, in depth as well as area, to find the greatest concentrations of feeding fish.

For best results, you must be equipped to fish the water in a variety of ways. First, you will need the drogues, clamp and a plank seat as already described, and then, to be able to fish the greatest volume of water and locate the trout effectively, three carbon rods with shooting-heads which will enable you to fish in water up to 50 feet deep:

- The 9-foot #8 general-purpose rod with 36 feet of ST #8 floating for surface work and 30 feet of ST #9 fast-sink for water up to 12 feet deep
- A 9½-foot #10 rod with 36 feet of ST #10 fast-sink and 30 feet of #11 extra-fast-sink for water up to 20 feet deep
- A 9½-foot #13 rod with 30-foot lengths of lead-core line weighing 375, 450 and 550 grains for water up to 50 feet deep (or more if necessary).

To avoid too many kinks in the backing, it is preferable to use two fly-reels of not less than 3⅝-inches diameter with at least 170 yards of 30-pound monofilament backing which is knotted to the loops on the ends of the shooting-heads with tucked half-blood knots, making line interchanging easy. Lines are best kept on the plastic spools on which they are supplied when not in use – carefully labelled, of course. All I do is cut off the fly, split the plastic spool, put the leader end under an elastic band encircling the spool, replace the other half of the spool, wind on the leader and line and then cut the backing knot outside the rod-tip. The next line can then be knotted on and unspooled. Let's have another day's fishing to see how best to use this tackle. . . .

Knowing I had the whole day, I'd booked a motor-boat, so 9 a.m. was starting time. The sun was already shining brightly, with occasional cloud and a gentle westerly breeze blowing into a corner of the reservoir formed by a natural bank to the right and a dam to the left, looking downwind. Conditions had been stable for at least three days, so it was likely that plenty of daphnia would be drifting into the area, with a plentiful supply of 'resident' food items in the weedbeds. The water here was nowhere deeper than 20 feet, so I decided to search it thoroughly with two outfits.

The first outfit was the 9-foot #8 rod with a 30-foot ST #9 fast-sink line, a 15-foot 8-pound leader and a bulky size 8 long-shank Black Tadpole. The fly was chosen on the premise that the line would not be fishing deeply, so fish looking up at the bright surface would have a good chance of seeing the black silhouette and lively tail.

But it was the second outfit in which I had more faith: the 9½-foot #10 rod with the 30-foot ST #11 extra-fast-sink line, since this would search a greater volume of water and the longer rod would lift the heavy sinking line from the water more effectively. The leader was 15 feet of 10-pound nylon with a size 8 long-shank Orange Tadpole.

Having checked the boat and stowed the oars which every boat should have (for emergency use). I went through my standard procedure for testing the motor. Is the tank full? Does the mechanism holding the propeller out of the water work properly? Does the motor start easily? Does it make any unusual noises? Does it stop and re-start easily? All was well!

It being mid-week, and approaching the main holiday season, not many boats were out and my chosen area was clear except for one anchored boat that could easily be avoided, so my ploy was to search the area systematically. Starting over the shallower water nearest the natural bank, I set a drift which would take the boat about 500 yards. Having raised the propeller out of the water, which I always do to avoid snagging the line or leader when a fish is in play, I attached the 3-foot square drogue's cord to the centre of the stern, beside the motor, and let the drogue over the stern, pulling to open it. Drifting slowly bow first, and directly down-wind, the drift would take me over water shallowing from 12 to 8 feet deep, according to the map in the fishery lodge. I placed the plank seat across the gunwales, half-way between the stern and first seat, and prepared the 9-foot rod for action with 25 yards of backing laid in the bottom of the boat.

Sitting facing the stern, but twisting to my right, I extended line with short shoots until I'd achieved the correct 3-foot overhang and followed up with a double-hauled forward cast to my right and square to the drift line (to the left side of the boat facing the direction of drift). This was easy because the breeze kept the ST line away from me as I cast. At the extreme end of the forward shoot, I gripped slightly with my left hand to brake the flow of backing, thus causing the line-end and leader to straighten about 30 yards away. Then, after letting 2 yards of backing run freely to allow the ST to sink, I retrieved with the slowest pulls possible, about one foot in 10 seconds, causing the fly to swing round high in the water until it was directly behind the boat.

At this point I speeded up the retrieve to pulls of about 2 feet per second until the backing knot was in my left hand. Then I made another cast, placing the fly 30 yards to my left, square to the line of drift. I achieved this by roll casting into the air to the right of the drogue, back-casting at 45 degrees to my right (in a downwind direction) with the rod almost horizontal, forward casting 45 degrees to my left (into the wind), and shooting enough line to create a 3-foot overhang. Then I back-cast square to my right, made a long forward shoot horizontally over the stern, square to the left, and, after letting go another 2 yards of backing, retrieved as before. I followed this with another cast square to the right – roll cast into the wind; back-cast over the bow with the rod tilted the usual 15 degrees; forward cast at 45 degrees to the right (into the wind) to create the overhang; back-cast at the same 45 degrees; and a long forward shoot square to the right.

That may sound all pretty boring stuff, but if it isn't followed correctly, the fly is likely to end up in your anatomy rather than on the water!

This time I had enough backing already pulled from the reel, so I allowed it to feed out through the rod rings so that the line sank uninfluenced for 10 seconds. Then backing and line were retrieved again, before I made another cast to the left with the same sinking time. I followed this with successive pairs of casts to right and left with sinking times of 20, 30 and 40 seconds, always feeding backing out so that the ST sank without influence. I varied the retrieve occasionally to include short, fast pulls. On the 40-second cast I felt a slight draw on the fly, but it was caused by a small piece of weed, so I knew that I was letting the line sink for too long. The fast-sinking ST belly was sinking at a known rate of 2.5 inches per second, so the depth was 2.5 inches × 40 seconds = 100 inches, or about 9 feet. The breeze was light, so the boat didn't travel far, even during the 40-second casts.

As no fish were showing, I decided to continue with a 30-second sinking time, which kept the fly clear of weed until I drifted over shallower water. Then I reduced the sinking times – 20, 15, 10 seconds, but all to no avail. The trout were either not there or didn't want the Black Tadpole. Though the drift was a blank, I covered an enormous amount of water deeply and effectively. An area 500 yards by 60 yards is just over 6 acres. A lure retrieved in this manner – slowly in a curved path, then speeding up towards the boat – can be particularly attractive to trout. The angler is in control of the fly at all times, and this method should never be confused with trolling.

With the drogue lifted, I motored back on an inshore curve (no bank anglers were about) to my starting 'line' (identified by a tree on one bank and an electricity pylon on the other) and then moved some 60 yards further offshore, with new 'marks' noted and the drogue re-set. The water was now deeper, so although I followed the same tactics, I did so with the 9½-foot rod and the 30-foot #11 extra-fast-sink line. The maximum depth of water was 20 feet, but without too much weed, so with a line known to sink at about 5 inches per second, my fly would reach this depth in 28 seconds. To see if any fish were shallower, or if the Orange Tadpole was preferred, I tried sinking times on either side of the boat of 10, 15, 20, 10, 15 and 20 seconds. Feeding out backing for the appropriate time soon becomes a habit, the only snag being the occasional tangle. However, this is likely only in a strong wind.

An interesting facet of this method is that the fly remains higher in the water than the ST belly as it sinks quickly. Then, when the backing is retrieved, the fly is drawn downwards in a curve. Trout seem at times to be particularly excited by this movement. Perhaps they think the prey, nearly in front of them, is about to escape, so they chase it and seize it violently.

Having drifted for about 200 yards and let the line sink inshore for about 20 seconds, I had just tightened the backing when I had a good, solid pull. I responded with a slow upward strike. The fish was obviously well hooked and bored steadily away, so I let the loose backing slide under steady pressure until it was tight to the reel. The fight wasn't spectacular, just a continuous powerful boring and circling which ended with a golden-flanked brown trout in the net. It weighed 3¼ pounds and had several snails in its stomach. By now the boat had drifted quite a long way, and my next inshore cast caught weed after 20 seconds, so it was time for sinking times to be reduced. However, no further takes were forthcoming.

Making the usual curved inshore return to my starting point, I considered making another drift on the same line, but rejected the idea on the grounds that brown trout are often solitary creatures at this time of the year. Accordingly, I moved a further 60 yards offshore and, as the breeze had increased a little, deployed my 5-foot square drogue to keep the boat still moving slowly.

The first cast, to my right, was easy, with the line blowing away from me and the horizontal cast to the left, over the stern, just possible in that the heavy #11 ST was not blown dangerously towards me. After letting the line sink for 20 seconds, I felt three 'tweaks' at the fly during the swinging retrieve, so, as the line straightened behind the boat, I started a fast retrieve of 3-feet per second. At the second pull a tremendous surge tore the backing from my hand and everything tightened so fast that the rod nearly went over the stern! The running battle that followed was really exciting, with a rainbow of 3¾ pounds eventually netted and found to have a stomach half-full of daphnia.

Good rainbows take some beating and a strong leader is essential when a heavy line is used. Some people are rather disparaging of this and suggest that a 6- or 7-pound leader would be more sporting. My view is that it is much more unsporting to be broken when using a weak leader (as will undoubtedly happen) than to use the relatively risk-free one of 10 pounds b/s.

The boat had again drifted a long way by the time I had boated and unhooked the trout, but I felt sure that more fish were in the area. Sure enough, after a 15-second sinking cast to the left, I had retrieved only half-way round when the fly was taken by a 1½ pound rainbow. This also contained a few daphnia. By now the dam was quite close, so I pulled in the drogue and made the usual curved return to my starting point. Once you locate a productive drift and depth, you should keep fishing it until sport ceases. Next time down, the same drift produced two more rainbows of 1¼ pounds and just over, but the following one brought only a half-hearted pull, then nothing. . . .

It was now nearly one o'clock and time for the local, but I thought I'd have one more drift. Otherwise I might have to wait until evening for more feeding trout. I moved the boat out a further 60 yards, but as the breeze was now stronger, the cast across the stern had become somewhat dangerous, with the fly being blown towards me. A change of style was needed: roll cast into the wind; back-cast over the bow; forward cast 45 degrees to my right (into the wind), to create the overhang; back-cast at 45 degrees; forward cast square to the right; and a long backward shoot to the left (to the right side of the boat facing the direction of drift). It is easy to cast backwards with the shooting-head, and the risk of my being hooked was eliminated, because the breeze kept the line away.

I allowed this cast to sink for 25 seconds, and no sooner had the backing tightened than I felt a good pull, then nothing. The thought crossed my mind that the fly was taken just as it was being pulled down, so, casting backwards again, I waited 25 seconds and then started a quick retrieve of about 2 feet per second, causing the fly to dive down fast. The result was positive and dramatic! That trout just didn't stop for 50 yards! The fight lasted for several minutes, but my mounting visions of a huge trout were dashed when another daphnia-feeding rainbow of only 1¾ pounds came to net. These relatively small fish that generate such power always amaze me. They're another good reason for using a 10-pound leader!

Having caught six fine trout in warm, bright weather, and still having time to eat before closing time left me with a sense of achievement – and the desire to experiment further. The real key to my success was that I had covered a lot of water, about 25 acres, and had located feeding trout by varying the sinking times of my fly.

The possible permutations are endless, should you have a year or two to spare! For instance, a floating ST with an 18-foot leader and a large, weighted nymph could be cast from a slowly moving boat, the backing fed out until the nymph was nearly on the bottom, and then retrieved slowly. This would cause the nymph to ascend attractively, in a smooth curve. Alternatively, a heavy line with a long leader and a buoyant Muddler Minnow could be cast from a quickly drifting boat to produce a sudden, downward curving dive, followed by a pulled retrieve, and so on . . . and on . . . and on. . . .

The deep-drifting method I have described can be used safely only by an angler fishing alone. A safer method when two anglers are in a boat is to drift with the drogue attached to the corner of the stern (*see page 119*) using the same heavy shooting-heads. The safe

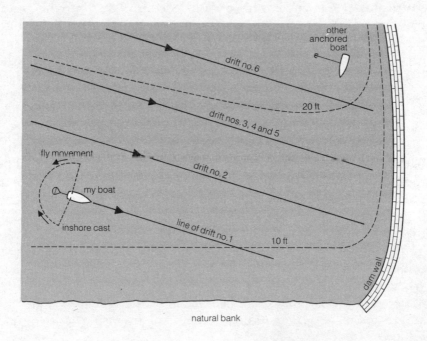

FIGURE 62: *Deep-drift plan*

casting angles will permit a reasonably wide band of water to be searched, which is important when fishing in difficult daytime conditions.

Alternatively, drift and sit as described for loch-style fishing (*page 120*), using 30-foot shooting-heads with sinking rates appropriate for the depth of water. Make your cast directly downwind, allow the line to sink, and fish the cast with a pulled retrieve. This is a good method to use as a prelude to loch-style fishing during the evening rise, and it has caught a significant number of 'bonus fish' for me. These trout are caught deep-down presumably because insect activity stimulates feeding well before any indication of it is apparent at the surface.

LATE JULY:
THE EVENING RISE

DESPITE THE vagaries of the British climate, sometime between early July and mid-September it will be hot. Whether the heat lasts for weeks or only days, almost certainly it will bring some good evening rises from the trout. These are caused by large numbers of insect pupae, usually of midges and sedges, moving to the surface to hatch – and the fish move with them. But the fishing is not always as easy as it seems it ought to be. Even experienced anglers suffer great disappointment in terms of fish caught, and some become almost frantic in their efforts to deceive the fish. The sight of an area of water appearing to boil as a result of trout movement quickens the pulse of even the dourest angler!

Some time ago I was able to fish an Essex water which had a marvellous evening rise, and the experience I gained there over four years convinced me most anglers can bring their knowledge and fishing methods almost to an art-form. Nature has organised things remarkably well. The pupae rise, hatch into flies which mate and lay eggs that sink to the bottom to turn into larvae and then into pupae, and the whole process is repeated. Indeed, it is all so well ordered that anyone who knows a water well can predict the time to start fishing with startling accuracy. It is this understanding of conditions, and the ability to fish with confidence, that brings consistent success in these circumstances.

For anyone who wishes to achieve this expertise, I would recommend that a start be made with a small trout lake – not larger than, say, 5 acres. The important features of these smaller waters are that plenty of fish will be within casting range, so the angler will maximise his opportunities; and that trout stocks are often high in relationship to the limited food supply, so the trout will feed more keenly when the chance of a meal comes along – and that may well bring about their downfall! This also applies to some large, relatively infertile waters. One well-stocked reservoir I know literally seethes with trout during the evening rise.

Fertile waters, and particularly large waters rich in daphnia, do not always produce such a frenetic evening rise. Sometimes it is good, but on other occasions it is underwhelming! This is perhaps understand-able, because any fish which has fed deep-down on an extensive daytime menu is unlikely to show the same enthusiasm for an evening dessert! Another problem on large waters is that the trout start to rise first over deep water, which is fine for boat anglers, but it is often some time before they are within reach of anglers on the bank, who may find that only the last hour before dark provides the chance of a fish, and then things are too hectic for them to gain a reasonably accurate impression of what is happening. Hence my recommend-ation to start on a small trout lake, where fish are likely to be within casting range throughout the evening.

What stimulates an evening rise? Put simply, what happens is this. During the heat of the day the insect larvae and pupae go about their business, feeding and resting in weedbeds and on the bottom. When evening comes, the cooler surface conditions stimulate the pupae, which begin to rise slowly and even to hover while they await suitable hatching conditions. Their movements attract the trout, which start to feed at levels yielding the best returns. Steadily the pupae ascend to higher levels and their numbers increase, and the trout follow them up. Then, as conditions reach their best, great numbers of pupae rise to the surface to hatch and, as hatching takes a little time if the surface tension of the water is strong, the trout take the chance to have a good feed, cruising along and sucking in the insects as quickly as they can, quite often with their noses breaking surface.

What a sight it is when hundreds of trout are feeding heartily in this way. The waters I usually fish have many more midges than sedges, and the fish seem to take each type broadly in proportion to the numbers hatching. As it becomes darker, and the atmosphere cools further, so the rise of insects tails off and the trout are no longer visible, but they continue to feed in mid-water for a short time. This suggests that some pupae are still coming up but, finding conditions not to their liking, then go down again to wait until early morning. The same hatching cycle happens again then, but mainly with midges and in a limited way.

A really good hatch of sedges has occurred on just two evenings while I have been fishing. The trout have seemed to follow their usual routine, and then have 'gone potty'. Not content with taking pupae in the surface film, they have swirled around, even chasing hatched adults skittering along the surface. This over-exuberance is out of character, and it must have been the movement of this much larger insect, in quantity, that was so provocative.

The trout see and suck in large numbers of very small food items with precision and in quite dark conditions, so their eyesight must be very good. The distance they can see must depend very much on light intensity and water clarity, but it would be unwise to underestimate their capabilities. Certainly the best demonstration of this I have seen was in a clear, calm river when I walked downstream and inadvertently into the view of a small shoal of sea-trout lying in 3 feet of water. They saw me at the same moment as I saw them, and the panic was total – at a distance of 40 yards in quite bright conditions. Experience on lakes and reservoirs leads me to believe that hatchery-bred trout are slightly less fearful of humans and movement than are wild trout, but that does not reflect on their eyesight, merely their upbringing.

Much has been written over the years about the trout's 'cone of vision' or 'window', which suggests that trout always look upwards for their food. In reality, this cone of vision refers to the trout's theoretical view of the outside world, as permitted by the laws of refraction. But this has little relevance to the trout angler during the evening rise. The trout's eyes are on the sides of the upper part of its head and although the front-end is a rounded taper, it must be able to see extremely well in front of its mouth to be able to feed as previously discussed. Why then should it not be able to see just as well upwards, sideways and to an extent backwards? The same question applies to downwards vision except there must be some reduction in this field of view, due to the bulk of the body. With these factors in mind I think of the trout as having a *sphere* of vision with a blind spot at the back and at the bottom. Without such a sphere of vision trout would probably be extinct by now due to attack by predatory fish. So what about the blind spots? Well, the trout only have to rotate their eyes a little, weave their heads from side to side, or tilt slightly on their vertical axis, in order to see in every direction. During the heat of day the sphere is at its largest with the top dazzlingly bright, but as the sun sets it becomes more comfortable to see upwards. As darkness approaches it would be reasonable to suppose that the sphere becomes progressively smaller, but not all that small – sea-trout can see a size 8 fly very near the surface from a depth of 6 feet in a river on a dark night.

But it is easy to imagine what happens during the first part of the evening feeding period. The trout may be cruising three or four feet down, quietly taking the first rising pupae coming up from below, picking them off at a convenient depth. With visibility still very good, the arrival of the fly-line on the surface above, or within, say, 6 or 7 yards, must be clearly visible to the trout and will probably frighten them. So it is better to cast infrequently, let the fly sink to an appropriate depth and then to retrieve slowly, giving the unseen fish time to cruise up to your offering and suck it in. You must watch your leader carefully, as there is seldom much indication that the fly has been taken. As more pupae ascend so the trout rise higher in the water, but looking below and sideways as well as forwards to see where the food is most plentiful, and they will move in virtually any direction to take it. Accordingly, your fly should be retrieved progressively closer to the surface until, ultimately, the trout are feeding right at the surface film and can be fished for individually because you can see where they are.

At this stage they seem less susceptible to slight surface disturbance, and it is possible to cast a line with a 9-foot leader and place the fly 2 feet in front of the trout without frightening it. This is presumably because it is concentrating on insects just in front of its nose and those it can see around it and rising from below. I used to be puzzled when I could plot the path of a trout, place my fly in front of it and not frighten or interest it, only to see it turn away to feed in a different direction. If it was unconcerned about the arrival of the leader and fly on the surface, how could it see and decide to turn to a more productive feeding area? The puzzle was solved only when I realised that the trout could see pupae coming up and thus decide which direction to take.

Trout feed generally in an upwind direction in a slight breeze, but will change direction frequently and deliberately. It is presumptuous of us to think they will go out of their way to take our clumsy imitations when so many naturals are about. However, an artificial drawn across a trout's nose only just under the surface may well be taken, and this is most easily achieved when the trout is moving in a predictable way – such as upwind. Movement is more random in calm conditions, and then it is difficult to place a fly accurately in front of a fish. In either situation it is easiest to cast a slow-sinking fly, such as an Invicta, accurately in front of and just beyond the trout, allow it to sink for a moment, and then to retrieve it. As a more accurate imitation of a pupa, a Pheasant Tail Nymph, which is less buoyant, could be cast further ahead and beyond the trout's path and allowed to sink for three or four seconds before being retrieved. The action of the retrieve should cause the leader to draw the fly in an upward curve, so that it is at the surface in front of the trout. If all goes well, it will be taken promptly. All too often it is not, because the whole sequence takes too long and the fish can easily change direction during the pause.

So evening-rise fishing is difficult because the trout are feeding at rapidly changing depths, often on two types of pupa which are present in great numbers, and on an erratic path. The most helpful feature is knowing that they are at least feeding!

Whenever I think about evening-rise fishing I recall one particular evening in August – typical of many, but remembered especially for its exciting conclusion – at my friend's Essex fishery (now sadly run down since my friend moved). The sun was already low in the sky following a really warm day, and there before me was the lake, roughly pear-shaped and about 150 yards long with a small island in the centre. The lightest of warm breezes was blowing from the narrow end, where two anglers were already fishing, so I made my way to a position opposite the island with the breeze coming from my left.

I had no premonition about this area. The previous evening had seen it produce an excellent rise, while other areas had much less activity. It was strange that even in so small a water, the trout were not evenly distributed. Why this was, I don't know, but obviously the fish did! A few small fish were moving here and there, but the general air was one of tranquillity. The short-cropped grass bank stopped at water only a foot deep, and the bottom gradually deepened to 6 feet before rising to the island. A light weedbed extended for about 4 yards to my right, with a few strands to my left.

To make the most of an evening's fishing, you need four leaders, which should be made up beforehand. They can be wound on any convenient spools, or even around your hat – anything that is at least 3 inches in diameter and smooth. The old-fashioned cast-holders are quite good, but the stepped periphery tends to put slight kinks in the nylon, which may cause tiny wakes in the water. This evening I had two leaders made up in exactly the same way:

9½ feet of leader and a 4-inch dropper of 6-pound nylon with a size 14 Olive Midge Pupa, and a 3-foot point of 5-pound nylon with a size 12 Olive Sedge Pupa. The third was 9 feet of 5-pound nylon with a lightly dressed size 12 Invicta; and the fourth, 9 feet of 7-pound with a size 10 G&H Sedge. Any leader nylon should be as clear as possible and glint-free, and this was Racine Tortue.

My first outfit was a 9-foot #7 carbon rod and WF #7 fluorescent-green line, to which was knotted one of the 12½-foot leaders by means of the tiny whipped loop at its end. These loops are invaluable during the evening rise, when quick changes of leader are needed to get the best results. The second outfit was a 9½-foot #7 carbon rod with a DT #7 fluorescent-green line and the 9-foot leader with the Invicta. The two unused leaders I wound on spools.

I prepared my first outfit by greasing the leader sparingly with Red Mucilin floatant for 4 feet, starting at the line loop. The remainder of the leader and flies were then degreased, together with my fingers. The sun was by now a red ball on the horizon, and still only the small fish were showing, so the Sedge and Midge Pupa combination fished 2½ feet down seemed ideal. I extended the WF head, which was 40 feet long, in the air until the back taper was just inside the tip-ring, and then made a final forward cast, shooting another 10 yards. This cast was straight across the breeze, which was now very light, and I could see the leader end going through the surface.

After about 15 seconds I started a slow retrieve of about one inch per second, with the line drifting slightly to the right, and then, when about 8 yards remained on the water, lifted it gently into a back-cast, followed by a false cast and shoot to position the WF head correctly, and then a final long shoot angled to the right. I let the flies sink for 20 seconds and then made another slow figure-of-eight retrieve as I watched the floating part of the leader intently. When the leader was still 8 yards beyond the weedbed, I saw it pulled slightly, which caused it to sink 2 or 3 inches more. I struck quickly, continuing to pull rapidly with my left hand. The water erupted and a small brook trout of about a pound took to the air like a Polaris missile, plainly on the point fly.

At this fishery I released all the trout I caught unless my friend needed some for the table, and this one was no exception. The way to do this without harming the fish is simple. Fish with the barbs on your hooks flattened with small pliers. Play the fish until it is very tired but not totally exhausted. Grip the rod between your right arm and side. Hold the leader with your left hand and draw the fish into the side. Slide your right hand down the leader, grip the fly and carefully twist the hook out in the opposite direction to that from which it went in. In most cases the fish will swim off immediately, but occasionally it will have to be held gently upright until it recovers.

Three casts later, in the same place, another fish drew the leader down quickly – a brown trout of about 2 pounds on the dropper. Two more casts produced nothing so I dried the leader with a cloth and then greased it as far as the dropper knot to bring the flies closer to the surface. I had my eye in now, and after letting the flies sink for 10 seconds, I made another slow retrieve. I had recovered only 3 yards when the leader twitched minutely and I struck: a rainbow of 1½ pounds, again on the dropper.

By now the sun had set and a few trout were beginning to feed at the surface, with their heads creating bumps in the surface film and occasionally a nose showing. These fish were feeding while swimming up what remained of the breeze, but swinging to one side or the other and then going down again. I removed and spooled the greased 12½-foot leader, degreased my fingers, and then knotted on the ungreased 12½-foot version – and degreased that, too! After hooking the new point fly in the keeper-ring and winding in the line, I put the 9-foot rod aside for use later.

Now I made the 9½-foot rod ready for action, degreasing the leader and Invicta and extending 18 yards of DT line in three shoots on to the water. Shortly afterwards a fish swam upwind about 15 yards out and to the right. Now the advantage that the longer rod and the fluorescent-green line (which could be seen clearly) gave me was that by drawing in enough line for the shorter range with my left hand, I could lift line off the water and aerialise it in one movement, and cast quickly to this fish. Unfortunately, this fish sank from view before the fly arrived.

However, another fish rose in front of me and stayed up, moving in a straight path at the same range, so I lifted the line into the back-cast again and cast forward to the fish. It was a little too long, the line landing next to the trout and sending it down in a big swirl.

Several fish appeared to the right, and one seemed to be maintaining a predictable path, so I waited until it reached the right distance and put the fly 18 inches in front of it and one foot beyond. After pausing for a moment, I drew the fly across its nose at about one foot per second, and it was taken immediately. I gently tightened by continuing the retrieve and lifting the rod and met a powerful resistance before a rainbow of about 2½ pounds took to the air. The tussle was a good one and this fish was netted for the table. It contained dozens of olive midge pupae, but no sedges, despite the fact that a few were hatching.

The commotion had not affected the other trout, which were feeding in even greater numbers. After two more abortive attempts, I managed to place the fly accurately and drew it in front of another fish. It was promptly taken. This was a 2-pound brown trout which I landed and released after a dogged fight. I noticed now how few fish were rising beyond the end of the island to my left or 50 yards to my right. There were some, but nothing like the numbers in my area.

I extended 18 yards of line again, which is essential if casting distance is to be gauged quickly. Speed is vital too, if the fly is to be placed precisely in front of the trout before it turns or goes down. This was even more important now as, with dusk advancing, the breeze had gone completely, with the result that trout were moving randomly. I spotted a fish to my right, and slightly nearer than my fly, which seemed to be maintaining a reasonably straight path while feeding purposefully, so I shortened the line, lifted off, changed direction and placed the fly in front and beyond. Following a slight pause to allow the Invicta to sink just below the surface, I drew it across the trout's feeding path and had it taken immediately. I had no need to strike, because the fish turned away and hooked itself.

To say that a commotion followed would be an understatement. It was a large fish and launched itself into several violent, twisting half-jumps before running up and down a 30-yard stretch of water. On three occasions it went straight through light weed and I could do nothing to stop it. Eventually it began to tire and circle in front of me, and then suddenly its resistance ceased and I was able to slide it over my small trout net. It was then that I had a shock, for the fish overhung each side of the net and was so heavy that I had to put the rod down, draw the net in and lift it over the low bank with both hands.

There on the grass, in the half-light, lay the most perfectly formed rainbow trout imaginable, with huge fins and an enormous girth. I could not bring myself to kill it, so it was weighed in the net in the light from a small torch which I always have to hand, and then carefully returned. After being held upright for several minutes, that magnificent fish, a shade under 6 pounds, swam slowly away.

I had taken at least 20 minutes to land this trout, and it was now too dark to fish on with the other rod with the ungreased leader and sinking pupae as I had planned. The trout had stopped rising and were probably well down, but now I could try something I had been thinking about for some time. Holding the little torch in my mouth, pointing away from the water, I exchanged the Invicta leader for the stronger G&H Sedge leader. This I cast straight in front and drew back quickly with 3-foot pulls every second, the fly making a tiny but visible wake. Another cast to the right produced nothing, but my next cast, to the left and fairly close to the bank, was another matter. The fly came quickly towards me, and suddenly was taken in an enormous swirl. The fight that followed in almost total darkness was one of the greatest determination and belligerence, and I really began to wonder what I had hooked. However, after five minutes all was revealed when a superbly marked brown trout of about 3½ pounds came over my net. I unhooked it in the torchlight and gently returned it to the water.

What a superb, never-to-be-forgotten evening's sport that was! Sometimes you 'get it right', but not always.

But after such good sport, it pays to note the important factors for future reference. On this occasion they were the following:

Settled, warm weather is needed for evening-rise fishing to be at its best. Even if the weather is good, a cool easterly breeze or a damp chill at dusk will kill the rise.

Pupae imitations should be retrieved very slowly before the rise starts, and you should be prepared to fish progressively nearer the surface as the evening advances.

A degreased leader minimises surface disturbance.

You may be surprised at the comparatively fast retrieve of one foot per second after the initial pause, but the fly must be kept at the right level and it will sink faster than you may imagine. My own experiment with those relatively slow-sinking and effective evening-rise flies, Invicta and Wickham's Fancy on 6-pound nylon, indicated approximate sinking rates of 3½ inches per second for a size 12, and 2¾ inches per second for size 14.

Accurate casting is vital, and in evening-rise fishing the target is moving, so the demands couldn't be greater. Casting practice at targets helps, but you must have the confidence to try, because your success rate will improve as you become more relaxed.

Where fishing is permitted after dark, a buoyant, wake-creating fly will sometimes interest trout, especially in warm, cloudy conditions, but don't try to fish one unless you have absolute confidence in your casting ability.

EARLY AUGUST:
RESERVOIR EVENING BANK-FISHING

I'VE ALREADY mentioned the difficulties associated with fishing a large reservoir at this time of year, a principal one being that the trout seem to feed within casting distance of the bank only in early morning or late evening, and then only in specific areas. A day-ticket angler who is not privy to this information may find the situation galling, but he should not be surprised. The boat angler is mobile and can seek the trout however deep they are feeding in bright, warm conditions, and wherever they are in a water. The bank angler is less mobile and is restricted to a narrow strip of water along perhaps several miles of bank, and is often hampered by weedbeds. So how does he select a productive spot?

Unless he has reliable and specific local information, the best advice is that he should undertake some reconnaissance, preferably on the evening before he is going fishing. Most reservoirs have strategically placed car-parks and often roads from which the water can be viewed. The numbers of anglers on a particular bank or cars in a particular car-park are good guides to where the action is, and a pair of binoculars allows fish-spotting. Given stable weather conditions, it is reasonable to expect trout to be present in the same general area 24 hours later. However, if a 'recce' is not possible, then a small water, where the best spot may be selected when the rise starts, is a better choice.

Some experienced season-ticket holders on large reservoirs have a different approach. They know which general areas are most productive, but not exactly which spot will produce the most prolific rise, because the fish do move about. They therefore time their arrival to coincide with the start of the rise, and then walk along their chosen length of bank watching for one or two rises close together and start fishing there. The idea is that if a few rises occur at the start, many more will appear when the full rise is in progress. It is a very successful system, provided you are prepared to work quickly for your fish. For my taste it is rather frantic. I prefer to arrive an hour or so earlier to fish slowly with sinking pupae imitations until the rise starts, then move a short distance if necessary.

With weather conditions stable, and having fished this reservoir four times in the previous 10 days, I felt optimistic about the prospects. The spot I selected was at the apex of a bay with almost straight sides at 90 degrees to each other, and with a light westerly breeze blowing out through its centre. A plantation of conifers enclosed the bay, but they were far enough away to allow a good back-cast and high enough to hide the setting sun. Overhead conditions had remained good, with a mixture of sunshine and cloud which looked likely to produce a warm dusk and, therefore, an excellent hatch of insects. The light ripple on the water began 20 yards out, where 5 feet of clear water lay over continuous weedbeds. The water had a good stock of fully acclimatised trout, though only the occasional fish was showing at least 100 yards offshore!

With an hour to go before sunset I took my time assembling two outfits chosen specifically to cope with the conditions previously experienced, where the trout stayed at least 20 yards out from the bank until dusk and thereafter came close in, often rising within a few feet of the small concrete dam wall on which I was standing.

My first outfit was the 9-foot #8 general-purpose carbon rod with a DT #7 fluorescent-green line and a 12-foot leader of 7½-pound nylon with a 4-inch dropper 3 feet from the point. The flies were both weighted but lightly dressed long-shank Gold-ribbed Hare's Ears, size 12 on the point and size 14 on the dropper.

The second outfit was a 9-foot #7 carbon rod, a DT #6 fluorescent-orange line and a similar leader with a size 14 Wickham's Fancy on the point and a size 14 Soldier Palmer on the dropper.

I had come one line-weight down in each case so as not to overload the rods when casting maximum distance – 30 yards – which is appropriate only for very experienced casters using the double-haul. Double-taper lines are best in this situation for precision casting and, more particularly, to ensure the leader turns over properly. A leader which fails to turn over is inclined to tangle, which is frustrating in the half-light when trout are rising all about you. The leader was on the heavy side to withstand the drowning effect of the long line and the risk of a fly attaching itself to weed during a fight.

I made ready with the 9-foot #8 rod, degreased the leader completely, and cast to maximum range, allowing the flies to sink to a depth of about 3 feet. Then I made a continuous figure-of-eight retrieve at a rate of about 2 inches per second into a line-tray. The line was fairly conspicuous on the relatively calm water, but the slow retrieve gave a trout plenty of time to swim to the flies without being put off by the line. Takes in circumstances such as this are extremely gentle, because the fish expects only to suck in an insect. The only time that a really positive indication is given is when a fish takes while moving away from the rod.

It is good sense to anticipate these gentle takes, particularly at long range where the leader cannot be seen clearly, and to take more positive steps than usual to hook the trout. In a normal strike, the rod is rotated from the wrist and/or elbow upwards, or sometimes sideways, which is not effective in this situation. This is because the rod-tip has to move radially quite a long way before it shortens the distance between the angler and fish and pulls the hook home (*see diagram below*). With this in mind, you may like to try the method of 'instantaneous striking' which I developed for sea-trout fishing at night.

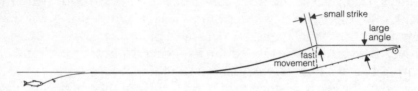

FIGURE 63: *Normal strike*

This rapid and effective strike is achieved by apparently leisurely movements, starting from a modified retrieving position for the rod hand. Instead of positioning your right elbow by your right side, push it forward so that your arm and rod are pointing down the line, almost straight from the shoulder, while your left hand is positioned over the line-tray as usual. A little more physical effort is needed to maintain this position, but it can be done in a relaxed manner and is not needed for a long period, anyway. When you suspect an offer, all you need do is draw your right elbow straight back past your side and then raise your rod-tip vertically from your elbow, at the same time drawing line sideways away from the rod, with your left hand. The net effect is that you shorten the line by at least 24 inches without using hurried movements, which is more than enough to take up any slack and to hook the fish. You may miss several trout when you fish this way, because their mouths are large in relation to the fly being used. This is particularly noticeable when a trout takes while moving towards you, since the hook often pulls straight out after being sucked in.

During the hour before sunset I caught four rainbow trout of 1¼–2¼ pounds and missed two others. All except one of the offers were gentle. The exception came when the trout must have taken the smaller fly while it was sinking ('taken on the drop'). This fish took powerfully while going away from me, which was clearly demonstrated when it made a porpoise-like leap immediately after being hooked. After several runs, it went through a weedbed and then became very sluggish. The reason for its inactivity was clear as I netted the fish: the leader had become festooned with weed which had slid down and covered the trout's eyes.

Many fish were rising out in the bay as dusk drew on, and one or two showed within casting range, so I changed to the lighter outfit. Shortly afterwards a trout showed, moving from left to right at about 18 yards, so I lifted off, cast the Wickham's in front of it and retrieved at the usual one foot per second. I was totally unprepared for what happened next, as the trout 'reared up' and came down on top of the fly without taking. I pulled again and, to my surprise, the trout did the same thing again, but this time taking on its way down. Unfortunately, I didn't notice the leader submerging until it was too late, but I didn't mind too much, since the incident had well demonstrated the trout's ability to see downwards. I caught two more trout by drawing the Wickham's across their noses, by which time a really good rise was in progress. Trout had gradually moved in and were showing everywhere, with some large fish among them. The strong nylon made good sense!

Spooning revealed that all the trout had recently eaten daphnia and midge pupae in varying proportions, which was usual for this water. However, it made me wonder whether daphnia (being light-sensitive) surface at dusk, and whether the evening rise is a combined one, so to speak.

An interesting sequel to this story occurred 12 days later, when, having returned from holiday, I decided on the spur of the moment to have an hour's fishing. I arrived at dusk in conditions similar to those I have described and headed for the same spot with the same Wickham's outfit. However, the rise was disappointing and limited despite the ideal conditions, and those fish that did show seemed to do so without enthusiasm. I had only four tweaks and missed them all! Somewhat puzzled, I was returning to the car-park when I met a solitary angler fishing near the entrance. He had caught four rainbow trout on a 2-inch White Lure fished just under the surface. My suspicions were aroused, as they were all fat stock-fish of a pound apiece. Then he said, 'Didn't you know? Five thousand were put in two days ago!'

Never was the contrast between the taking habits of fully acclimatised fish and stock-fish more clearly demonstrated. Had I made time to visit the fishery lodge beforehand, I would have known about the stocking and anticipated the possibilities. Anyway, for the next three weeks there was little point in fishing with anything other than a neutral-density line and a 7-pound leader with a size 10 White Tadpole on the point and a similar-size Black Tadpole on the dropper. Scores of trout went into my bag, and I was rather glad when the remaining stock-fish became acclimatised and fully responsive to imitative flies.

LATE AUGUST: AN UNUSUAL RESERVOIR DAY

THE FISHING DAY I'm about to describe has something in common with the experiences related in the last chapter, but with subtle differences. Following its opening, this reservoir was lightly stocked with trout in April. Large numbers of coarse fish were present, and in those early days, especially in summer, it was difficult to catch trout. Any success was well earned, and this particular day was no exception. The weather was warm and I had toiled all morning on the dam wall with a heavy split-cane rod and a sinking DT line, thinking that the deep water would provide the best chance, but it yielded not an offer.

A walk along the shallow natural bank seemed a good idea, if only to relieve the monotony, despite the fact that I had only wellington boots, and thus couldn't wade. But at least my new DT floating line could be used to good effect, as the water was too shallow for the sinker. The leader was 10 feet of 6½-pound nylon with a size 12 Ivens Green Nymph attached. After I had walked about 250 yards along the bank, there was an explosion of silver roach fry, and then another only 10 yards out. I couldn't believe my eyes! Action at last! I quickly cast in the area of activity and retrieved my nymph slowly, though with little conviction. But I hadn't had time to change to a lure. Suddenly a moving hump showed on the surface to my left, preceded by a shimmering furrow of fry. I cast my nymph directly in front of the hump, left it for a second, and then retrieved sharply at about 2 feet per second. It was taken instantly and, after an unspectacular but persistent fight, a brown trout of 3¾ pounds came to net. It had eaten so many fry that they were even showing in its throat.

With no further activity along the natural bank, I returned to the dam wall in the hope that some trout might rise later. In fact, I had a good rest until almost sunset, when a few trout started to rise within casting range. None of the insect imitations I offered them created the slightest interest. In truth, I couldn't see any insects, but assumed that some must be hatching. As a last resort, I tied on a 2½-inch Grey Lure with tandem hooks, cast and retrieved quickly at about 3 feet per second. The lure was seized after a few minutes and I duly landed a 2-pound rainbow which had been feeding only on daphnia, with no trace of insects in its stomach. Shortly afterwards I felt another pull, but missed – and then the rise was over.

The capture of that brace of trout gave me a lot of pleasure, as I'd overcome difficult conditions, but the manner in which they were deceived was interesting. Are we to assume that the brown trout, while gorging boringly plentiful fry, stopped for a succulent, savoury nymph? Are we also to assume that the daphnia connoisseur could be tempted only by a 'whitebait'? Anomalies like these occur frequently in fishing, and we'll probably never know the explanations. But to know they exist and to understand the advantages of trying 'opposites' is enough.

LATE AUGUST: RESERVOIR DAPPING

VISITING AN old friend in the West Country for a long weekend, I was able to organise a day's fishing on a large reservoir nearby. It was arranged that I would fish in the morning, go back for lunch, then fish again until early evening, so to make best use of the limited time available, I booked a motor-boat. The summer had not been good and this August day showed no improvement, being mild but overcast and windy. I spent an eventful morning fishing loch-style (*pages 120 to 124*) and by lunchtime needed only two trout to make a limit.

Lunch brought a surprise. My host's son, Andrew, arrived unexpectedly and, hearing that I was fishing, announced that he had always wanted to catch some trout. Not *one* trout, mark you, *some* trout! What was I to do? Having insufficient time to teach him how to cast and fish, my only option was to take him dapping. This age-old method of fishing can be exciting and productive on stillwaters, given sufficient wind – so at least the weather was suitable. The skills needed can be learned in minutes, but would the trout co-operate?

I put up a 15½-foot telescopic carbon dapping rod that I usually keep in the car boot with a shooting-head reel, loaded with braided nylon backing with a looped end. To this I attached a 15-yard length of medium dapping blowline with loops at both ends, and then a 3½-foot 10-pound leader. Traditional dapping flies are many and varied, but I find an artificial size 10 Daddy-long-legs the most successful on lowland reservoirs, and I always have at least six of these with me in a small fly-box, always pre-treated with Red Mucilin so that they will float properly. Done gently, this means that the flies are ready for instant use. Having knotted one on to the leader, I telescoped the rod down and wound the line in until the hook was in the tip-ring, which is large. This does no harm to the fly if done with care, and avoids doubling the leader over the tip-ring, which may cause an irritating kink in the nylon.

Equipped with his ticket and a rod licence, my new partner embarked full of expectation and we motored across to the area I had been fishing in the morning. Here the wind swept down over extensive grass banks before creating a good ripple on the water, and my reasoning was that feeding trout would be heading upwind and taking any insects being blown offshore. I took care to come in from the side of the first drift line because the trout have had plenty of frightening experiences with boats by the time August arrives. Dapping is a good method for the same reason, because the angler uses minimum movement when controlling the fly and the fish tend to come closer to the boat. My plan was that Andrew would dap sitting astride the higher bow seat, where he could see better, and I would fish from the stern, loch-style, casting only when a trout was seen rising within range. This gave me plenty of water to cover, but ensured that the fish would come within 6 or 7 yards of the boat without seeing any disconcerting movements. As I am right-handed, I had the boat drift square to the wind with me to the right of the drogue looking downwind.

With the boat ready, Andrew extended his rod fully in my direction and held it horizontally so that I could remove the fly from the tip-ring and then pull out the leader and 10 yards of blow-line to be laid in the boat. While I held the fly, Andrew now raised the rod to the vertical, holding it with both hands; the wind blew the line out, and when it pulled the fly, I let go. The point of this operation is to keep the line dry, so it will 'fly' well, and this one certainly did.

With the rod vertical, the fly was off the water, so Andrew lowered it until the fly danced and skittered backwards and forwards on the water. It didn't take long, or much advice, before Andrew had the fly dancing on the water 12 yards out. If the wind dropped, he raised the rod to increase the wind resistance of the line; if it gusted strongly, he lowered it. After a few minutes more he found that moving the rod-tip from side to side gave greater variation. I was fascinated to watch a newcomer at work, and it was not long before a trout boiled at the fly. Andrew lifted the rod immediately, and I couldn't see if the fish had taken the fly or not, but the excitement was tremendous! My advice was quiet but precise: 'Wait until you see the leader being pulled, then strike gently.' After ten minutes or so another trout came 'from nowhere' and took the fly, but Andrew was too quick. The hook just pricked the trout's mouth on its way out, provoking a great leap from the fish.

Nothing happened for some time in spite of some deft fly control which kept the new angler totally absorbed. Then suddenly there was a boil, and the leader just kept going down, followed by a rather hesitant strike that set the hook. The reel screamed in protest as the trout set off on a good run away from the boat. This was ideal, because beginners often try to bring the trout in close too soon, and lively fish go under the boat, which can be awkward. Luckily, the fish circled and bored well away from us, then appeared to yield. This caused Andrew to make his one, and nearly fatal, mistake: he started to wind in. Suddenly the trout turned tail and ran again, but Andrew forgot to let go of the reel handle. The rod was pulled down to the water, with the 10-pound leader and hook-hold strained to . . . well, no, not quite breaking point, but it must have been close! With the handle released, the reel turned at great speed, and it was fortunate that I'd increased the ratchet strength, for it prevented an overrun. After this it was plain sailing and a rainbow of just over 2 pounds came to net, leaving Andrew overjoyed and slightly shaky.

I tied on a new Daddy-long-legs to replace the successful but now bedraggled one, and Andrew let the line blow in the wind to dry. It was time to start a new drift, too, because we were now a long way offshore. Taking my usual curved course to avoid our drift line, I took the boat back to our starting point.

Andrew now had good control of the line and had more or less mastered the art of keeping just the fly on the water, rather than some of the leader as well, so I left him to his own devices while I scanned the water for a rising fish. Suddenly there was a hearty splash at the 'Daddy', followed by Andrew saying a fish had whacked the fly with its tail. This happened again shortly afterwards, but then it was my turn. I saw a fish approaching at the surface some 20 yards away beyond the stern. I waited, then cast into its path at 10 yards range, and after a quick retrieve had my point fly taken. A rainbow of just over 1½ pounds eventually came to net. As I was dealing with it, I heard a swirl, then 'Got him!' Andrew was more professional this time, keeping his rod up and letting go of the reel handle in good time when the fish ran. He couldn't stop the fish going under the boat at the finish, but the rod was passed round the bow and the fish netted on the drogue side. This always offers the danger of snagging, but all went well and a 1¾-pound rainbow came aboard with its proud captor looking more composed than he had after his first fish.

We fished on for a while, but with no more rises to the dap, we motored back to start a new drift on a different line. The wind was moderating slightly now, so Andrew held the dapping rod-tip higher to increase the pressure on the blowline. It wasn't long before I heard a mighty splash and another, 'Got him!' This rainbow seemed more intent on doing the 110-metres high hurdles than anything else, but eventually went quiet and came over the net. It weighed exactly 3 pounds and was in 'the pink' of condition. Now the wind was really dropping and the blowline would hardly 'fly', but conditions were beginning to suit me more and it was not long before I caught my last trout to make a limit.

My young friend's excitement when we returned home can be imagined: 'My three to Mike's two!' But there was no doubt that it was the dapping equipment that made the day!

The angler wishing to take dapping seriously has a number of interesting aspects to explore. Various flies can be used to imitate different food items likely to be found on the surface, for example a G&H Sedge or a heavily dressed Black Zulu might be taken as a bee or a bluebottle. He should remember, too, that a strong wind will blow all sorts of trout food on to the water, such as butterflies and ants, so it pays to keep a careful watch.

Dapping probably brings more abortive offers than any other form of fly-fishing, so the right selection of fly on a particular day can make all the difference. Some fishery managements allow the use of natural insects, but I can't be bothered to collect them. In strong, gusty winds, a long-shank size 6 nymph of any type can be used on the point as an anchor, with the dapping fly attached to a dropper perhaps 18 inches up the leader.

I don't do much dapping, but I usually take a medium dapping line with me which is made of about 120 strands of Crimplene, all knotted together every 2 feet. There is scope for experiment here, and buying a large reel of Crimplene will allow you to make larger – and smaller – diameter lines for use in different wind strengths. Finally, it is important to remember the effect of the drogue on the way the line behaves. In a light wind, a 5-foot square drogue will slow the boat and increase the wind speed acting on the line, whereas in a strong wind a 3-foot square drogue will increase the speed of the boat and decrease the wind speed on the line. This method is the norm on many Irish and Scottish lochs when there is enough wind, and there is plenty of scope for its development on our lowland reservoirs.

LATE SEPTEMBER:
RESERVOIR BANK-FISHING

'Wind from the west with bright spells and showers, heavy at times,' said the weather forecaster, but rain means nothing to a properly clad fisherman! I arrived at the reservoir at about 9.30 a.m. during a bright spell, as luck would have it, and found a favourite stretch of bank unoccupied. This was a straight, sloping beach of clay and stones, 200 yards long and 30 yards wide, which had been exposed by a 6-foot drop in water level. A moderately strong wind was blowing from left to right and offshore at an angle of some 45 degrees – ideal for the bank fisherman. Some sparse weed-beds were being stirred up and their insect populations disturbed, but the ripple was enough to conceal my presence reasonably well from the fish. Many trout seem to move inshore with the onset of cooler weather, possibly because daphnia become scarcer. They forage in the weedbeds and on the bottom for insects and snails in water 6-feet deep or more, with the occasional foray into shallower water to harass shoals of fry; but they do not stay long for fear, it seems, of aerial attack. Under these conditions I again used two outfits: the 9-foot #8 general-purpose carbon rod with a 38-foot head WF #8 neutral-density line, a 12-foot leader of

7-pound nylon and a size 12 Silver Invicta; and a 9-foot #9 carbon rod with a 39-foot head ST #9 medium-sinking line, a 12- foot 8-pound leader and a size 10 Grey Muddler Minnow.

It was already looking showery, so I pulled on my waders and attached their straps to my belt, followed by a pair of waterproof over-trousers cut off above the knees. Then I put on a breathable waterproof coat with its hood press-studded on over a towelling scarf just crossed over under my chin. Having to wear spectacles, I used to find fishing in the rain a miserable experience, so I had my coat hood modified with a doubled piece of waterproof material stitched on the front to produce a horseshoe-shaped peak 3 inches long. I pull the hood on over my cap and my spectacles are kept dry unless I have actually to face into driving rain. However, hoods deaden sound, so I pull it up only when really necessary.

Having buckled my line-tray around my waist and hung a folding net on my belt, I took the 9-foot #9 outfit and waded carefully out for about 10 yards from the centre of the straight beach. Long casting can be tiring, but I really enjoy an hour or so at it because hooking at a fish at long range is especially satisfying. But remember, the 39-foot head can be cast only by an experienced angler using good double-haul technique. A fisherman not using double-haul will do better with head-lengths of 32–36 feet, depending on his ability.

Unhooking the Muddler from the keeper-ring, I made casts of increasing length both in front and at an angle to the right to make sure that any fish close in were not frightened by the line. A straight, level back-cast is essential if a good fishing distance is to be achieved, and on this occasion it was easy because my back-cast was totally unobstructed.

I retrieved the backing end of my line until it reached my hand, then I rolled the line into the air and made one back-cast. On the first forward cast I allowed a short shoot to take the ST 3 feet outside the tip-ring, then made a gentle level back-cast followed by a rapidly accelerated forward cast at a slightly upward angle. With the help of a semi-following wind and a narrow casting loop, the leader straightened to place the fly at least 40 yards away.

Most anglers rely too much on physical strength when they try to cast a long line, forgetting that powerful movements are slow. It is the steady build-up of speed, finishing with the flick and abrupt stop, that causes the rod to recoil with great speed. Remember the paint-brush exercise (*page 23*) and the fact that the rod-tip will not be pulling more than 4 ounces of dynamic weight during the cast.

Because the rod will not accept a greater loading than this at the tip, there is absolutely no point in putting extra effort in at the handle end.

I allowed the line to sink for 10 seconds and followed on with a pulled retrieve of 2 feet per second with slight pauses in between. Being buoyant, the Muddler spent the first two pulls on and just under the surface (movements which are attractive to trout at times) and then tended to keep just above the bottom weed as the line sank.

After perhaps 15 minutes I had a powerful take which high-lighted the need for a strong leader. I played the trout 'by hand', pulling backing in and dropping it into the line-tray, or releasing it under tension as necessary. You have to be careful not to burn your hands if you play fast-running trout in this way, but you will usually land fish more quickly. It seems to me that trout particularly dislike the vibration of the reel ratchet which is transmitted down the line, whereas playing by hand is 'softer'. It's a useful method should you hook a large fish on a light leader or small fly.

Larger-than-average fish can be expected at this time of year, and this rainbow weighed 3¾ pounds even though it had an empty stomach. No time must be lost after a fish is landed, because a shoal may have arrived. Sure enough, my second cast after I'd waded out again produced an even more powerful take. Sadly, this fine trout jumped about 30 yards away and threw the hook! However, the next cast produced a much more gentle take, and I eventually landed another rainbow of 2¼ pounds with a few midge pupae in it. After a further uneventful 20 minutes, it seemed that the shoal had moved on, so I decided on a change of tactics.

It was dull and raining quite hard by now, and I thought that the trout might now come closer, because they would feel less threatened from above in the poor visibility. It seemed appropriate to try a more gentle presentation with the 9-foot #8 outfit. After wading out again, I used my normal tactics of extending line gradually, with each cast retrieved in gentle pulls of around 3 inches per second. I had every confidence in my Silver Invicta (which, I'm sure, is taken as a caricature of both insects and small fish), but it must have been half an hour before an offer material-ised. This fish was a brown trout of 1¾ pounds which had several fry in its stomach, and the take came at the very end of the retrieve. This did not really surprise me. Of the six rises I had noticed that morning, all had been close in and two were closer to the beach than I was! The same fly deceived another fry-feeding rainbow of 2¼ pounds before the sun came out again and it was bright and warm for a time.

Thinking that the trout might be further out in deeper safer water, I switched back to the 9-foot #9 outfit, but not before I'd re-knotted the fly as a precaution. Someone once said, 'Expertise is brought about by an infinite capacity for paying attention to detail,' or something like that. Well, I keep trying! It is important, too, to check the leader frequently for knots, since long casting with shooting-heads is likely to cause more than is usual with other lines. Night-fishing for sea-trout has taught me to listen carefully, and I can often hear when a significant knot has formed.

To cover as many fish as possible, I now cast to maximum range and retrieved as before, but taking a pace to the left while the line was sinking. Moving upwind tends to lengthen the cast, but great care should be taken with foot movement. In this case the bottom was firm, so no discolouration of the water occurred, but clouds of mud are produced when the bottom is soft. It's as well to remain stationary when this happens, otherwise the coloured water may drift into the area being fished, which the trout will then avoid. After a further 10 minutes I felt a 'tweak' at long range, so I speeded up my retrieve. After another 10 yards I had a firm take. This is a useful ploy to make a hesitant fish take. It seems to arouse its predatory instincts to the full. This rainbow weighed just over 2 pounds and contained four red bloodworms (midge larvae) and two snails.

Having moved as far upwind as the point of the next bay without another offer, I waded carefully from the water and walked downwind for 150 yards, waded in again and started casting. On my second cast the shooting-head had just come into the rod rings when the Muddler was taken at short range. The solid *tug, tug* and bore-and-circle characteristics of this fight suggested I was attached to another brown trout. So it was – a 2¼-pounder with several fry in its stomach.

So what conclusions can be drawn from this day's fishing? It was important to select a bank known to be attractive to trout and where they could be expected to be moving along to feed, so personal experience or good local information is clearly a great help when fishing on large waters. Earlier in the season this bank had produced only rainbows, but brown trout appeared in some numbers towards the season's end. It seems, then, that they stay in deep water during the summer and move into shallower water only when it cools down. Perhaps, too, they come in to move along the shore in search of a spawning stream. One reservoir I know has such a stream in which large brown trout are trapped every year to provide ova for the hatchery. Rainbows do the same thing, despite the fact that they are unlikely to breed there. So the lesson is never to ignore the attraction of a small inflow of water to trout at the end of the season.

I derive much of my pleasure in trout fishing from the physical activity involved in casting, and there is no better time to improve your performance than when you are wading. Don't be put off! Not all the fish are 35 yards out. Use your 30-foot shooting-head and maintain a good style, and your distance will improve. But don't expect good results when the weather is bright and the water shallow. Last but not least, remember that a slow- sinking shooting-head and a semi-buoyant fly will help you to keep out of weed and will create less surface disturbance as well.

LATE SEPTEMBER: RESERVOIR BOAT-FISHING AT GREAT DEPTH

THE USE OF very heavy lines for trout fishing doesn't fit every angler's idea of fly-fishing. Sometimes, however, such a line is a basic necessity if any fish at all are to be caught or, more occasionally, a specific group of trout is to be confronted. By very heavy lines I mean 30-foot lead-core shooting-heads weighing 350, 450 or 550 grains, or a 36-foot ST #12 extra-fast-sinking line. The shorter lead-core lines (*pages 124 to 131*) have the fastest sinking characteristics, and the longer #12 the greater distance potential.

A powerful rod is needed if these heavy lines are to be cast efficiently; it should also be reasonably long to remove extra- fast-sinking lines from the water. A rod of 9½ feet is long enough for most people, given the leverage and line weight involved; longer rods are bound to be more tiring. The rod action should be similar to that described for the 9-foot #8 carbon rod (*page 28*) and when tested in the same way, a 9½-foot #13 carbon rod should deflect 7 inches with a 550-grain line hung on its tip-ring. I have used so-called lead-core rods which had butt actions, but these were about as useful as sticks of liquorice. They 'flopped' out a line with a large loop, when what was really needed was a reasonably narrow loop and a good line speed.

Most large reservoirs have draw-off towers, and these are excellent ambush points for predatory trout. One particular water has a large tower connected by walls to the main dam, and the corners thus formed always held large shoals of fry. Although only lightly stocked with brown trout at the time, they would move inshore from mid-September onwards to join a good stock of rainbows feeding at the foot of the tower. To judge from the sporadic bouts of panic displayed by the fry at the surface, these hunters enjoyed breakfast, lunch, dinner and snacks in between by attacking from below. The best place to catch them was along the front of the tower and close to the bottom, at a depth of about 30 feet, where they seemed to lurk between feeding excursions. A day spent there is worth description.

I chose my 36-foot ST #12 extra-fast-sinking line because its sinking rate was fast enough to approach the bottom in about one minute, but not so fast as to keep on sinking to the bottom while it was being retrieved, which is what would happen with a lead-core. Also, the 36-foot length was needed to cast the 40 yards to the far corner of the tower. This may sound a long way, but with a very heavy line, practice and a good technique, it is not too difficult to achieve. I could have used a 30-foot lead-core, but short lead-core lines cannot be cast long distances tidily and need heavy braking on the backing to straighten them.

Fly colour needs consideration when you fish in such deep water. A friend who goes diving in reservoirs confirms that, in average water clarity, red, green and blue show up as nearly black at depths such as we are considering, whereas yellow and white appear as shades of grey. He established this by looking at large, specially tied flies mounted in a wire frame. But fish are sensitive to vibrations, which enables them to locate food at great depths, so a good proposition seems to be to present them with a large white fly, somewhat like a fry but with plenty of 'flutter' and bulk to cause vibrations. My choice for the location I have described was a size 6 long-shank all-white Muddler Minnow with wide silver ribbing and a long marabou wing. Since it is essential to use strong leaders to avoid cracking off such large flies (lures?) in casting, rather than to deal with the strength of the trout, I chose to use a 12-foot leader of 10-pound nylon.

Having looped my ST to 100 yards of 25-pound braided nylon backing on a 3¾-inch diameter reel mounted on my 9½-foot #13 rod, and tied on the fly, I made the usual safety checks and rowed the boat to the tower. To be able to fish the area well in the slight onshore wind, I had to moor the boat about 15 yards upwind from the tower and 5 yards further out than the offshore face. Being on my own, I found it best to row the boat some 50 yards upwind, ship the oars, drift downwind and drop the anchor. Once the anchor had bitten into the bottom, I could let out more rope until the boat was correctly positioned. Then I tied the anchor rope to the bow to present minimum wind resistance.

I aerialised my ST and made a gentle cast of about 30 yards to just in front of the tower, allowing the line to sink for 50 seconds while I paid out backing to prevent the line tightening and sinking along a radius from the rod-tip, thus shortening the fishing distance. I then retrieved line with steady pulls of one foot per second until the ST reached my hand, and followed up with two roll casts to bring the line to the surface and position it in the air in front. Making successive casts of the same length, I allowed an extra 5 seconds' sinking time for each. At 70 seconds I felt a dragging resistance and my fly came back with little pieces of black debris from the bottom on the hook-point.

Having established the time needed to reach the bottom, I made several casts with sinking times of 60 and 65 seconds, but without response. Pulling an additional 5 yards of backing from the reel, I made a longer cast with a crisper final flick and faster left-hand haul. Allowing 65 seconds' sinking time, I had just started the retrieve when I felt a powerful tug. I struck upwards and connected with a strong fish. Trout hooked at great depth are often quite difficult to bring to the surface, unless they swim up of their own accord. Their body shape and fins allow them to resist an upward pull very well. However, after five minutes I was able to net a splendid brown trout of 3½ pounds which had several partly digested fry in its stomach.

Three more brown trout and two rainbows, all 2¾–4 pounds, came to net on that memorable morning. My casts were both long and short, with frequent breaks so that the trout were not alarmed by the line being dragged past them continually. No, it's not the most elegant fishing, but if large brown trout are your quarry, then this is often the way to catch them.

Towers are not the only places where deep-lying browns will be found, particularly early in the year. Deep-water exploration with a plumb-line may well locate steep banks or channels which can be fished in the same way, and I have reasonable success with rainbows in the same manner in hot weather. Given a clear bottom, it is worth letting the line settle for a minute and then retrieving very slowly. Takes occur most frequently early in the retrieve or just as the fly is leaving the bottom in an upward curve.

Some anglers specialise in fishing in this manner for large trout, and they have taken double-figure specimens. Frankly, apart from the pleasure of casting a really long line, I don't now enjoy this deep-water fishing as much as I did, and I rarely practise it. But provided the method is within the rules, and you find it to your liking, go ahead. It is the variation in the ways that trout can be caught with a fly that makes the sport so enjoyable.

The tackle I have described is for the specialist using distance-casting techniques, but don't be put off if you are inexperienced but feel like trying the method on a very bright day. Use your general-purpose rod – say, the 9-foot #8 – and equip yourself with a 30-foot ST #9 extra-fast-sinking line (which the rod should cast well) and a size 10 White Muddler Minnow. You will need patience while the line sinks, but it will make less disturbance near the fish, which may compensate for your reduced casting range and the less visible fly. Should you be lucky enough to catch an enormous trout in this way, you will have something to remember for life!

LATE OCTOBER: RESERVOIR BANK-FISHING

IT WAS AN unpleasant afternoon, continuously overcast with heavy showers and a strong, chilling south-easterly wind. With the season's end approaching fast, I decided to spend a final couple of hours fishing, though I hardly expected to catch trout in the cold conditions.

My choice of bank was easy: a nice straight stretch near the car-park, with the wind coming from left to right and slightly offshore. The water was no more than 6 feet deep within casting range, but I felt sure that some trout would be swimming upwind to join some semi-residents that were attacking small shoals of fry. Two anglers had already taken the best places at the upwind end of the bank, which had some shelter. They were fishing with floating lines and teams of three flies, but the fish had not been co-operative. They were casting short lines at 45 degrees downwind and using very slow retrieves, so their flies were not dragging too badly.

Because I wanted the easiest casting possible in the rough conditions, I chose my 9-foot #8 rod and, thinking the trout would be deep, due to the cold, my 36-foot ST #8 neutral-density line.

My leader was 10 feet of 7½-pound nylon and my fly a size 10 White Tadpole to imitate the fry.

Wading out about 30 yards downwind of my neighbour, I gradually extended line, which I retrieved into my line-tray (essential in that wind). A pulled retrieve of about one foot per second was necessary to prevent the fly hooking the bottom weed, but after only five minutes I had a strong take. My two neighbours hooked trout at almost the same time, which suggested a shoal had moved through. My fish was particularly vigorous and continued to run downwind, so far in fact that I had to leave the water and run to follow it. At one stage it was wallowing on the surface 60 yards out, although it didn't seem particularly large. Eventually I beached it (having left my net behind) – a rainbow of 2½ pounds with a few daphnia in it – at least 70 yards from where it was hooked. It was an incredible performance, and just went to show that weak leaders have no place when fishing waters of this type.

Beaching a trout is an excellent alternative to netting where clay or shingle slopes gently into the water. The fish should be played to exhaustion, and then drawn towards the bank into very shallow water. It will turn on its side as it grounds, and then a steady pull from a well-bent, horizontal rod will slide it out of the water. Any small 'flops' from the fish will help the sliding action. It is wise, once it is out of the water and still, to walk behind the fish and push it up the slope a safe distance before you use the priest. I once found a friend contemplating suicide, having beached a sizeable salmon, removed the hook and then seen the fish 'come to life' and regain its freedom!

After a further half-hour's fishing, with only one slight pull for encouragement, I went back to my car to warm up. The angler first in line had packed up, when I returned, so I moved into his place to take advantage of the slight shelter. During that last hour I had seven offers, but landed only two rainbows. Both contained a few daphnia and dark-brown midge pupae. But the important point is that my neighbour had four offers and caught three fish with his floating line and size 12 nymphs. In spite of the cold, his flies were attracting the fish to the surface and, although there was no evening rise as such, the trout seemed to be responding to increased insect activity.

My problem was that having chosen the very slow-sinking line, I had to retrieve it fast enough to prevent the fly snagging the bottom weed. However, this moved the fly too quickly across the path of the fish. As a result, they were just 'tweaking' the fly, and not deviating from their feeding path to take firmly. A floating shooting-head cast 45 degrees downwind would have allowed a much slower retrieve, allowing the trout to suck in the fly in a more leisurely fashion. However, that line was in my car, and by the time I had realised what was going on, it was too late to change.

This all goes to show that the angler should have floating and sinking lines ready for immediate use even in adverse conditions. He should also be prepared to retrieve slowly to catch fully acclimatised fish in cold conditions. My only consolation was that, in spite of my poor catch-to-offer ratio, I had enjoyed the best fight of the season!

CONCLUSION

To ATTEMPT to summarise several thousand words on different methods of fishing for stillwater trout in a few sentences may seem ambitious, but really only three main factors need to be considered.

- Locate the fish. They can be localised even in a very small water.
- Use appropriate equipment. This will vary from water to water and with the time of day or year, but it must enable the angler to position his fly correctly in relation to the trout and its feeding mood.
- Select a fly the trout will take. Fly selection is by no means an exact science, and what seems to be an odd choice may often 'work' well. However, it may not seem so odd once an informed assessment is made, particularly after a marrow spoon has been put to good use.

The various methods of fishing I have described are not the only techniques that might be successful on a given day. For instance, while loch-style fishing from a boat is producing fish in May, bank-fishing could be just as rewarding. But in other situations, such as at the evening rise or in daytime fishing when it is hot, to use the wrong method is to guarantee frustration.

Specialised Tackle

I HAVE ALREADY given a general idea of what tackle is needed to meet fairly specific needs. In particular, I have dealt in detail with the 9-foot #8 carbon rod and the various types of fly-line because they are the most important items for beginners. However, I have given scant attention to many other items and, indeed, ignored others altogether. But this is as it should be, to avoid each chapter resembling a tackle catalogue! I hope that what follows will remedy my sins of omission.

RODS

MY PREFERENCE for a 9-foot rod for general-purpose fly-fishing is plain. It is by far the most versatile, accurate and least tiring rod to use. The introduction of carbon-fibre in particular has seen a steady increase in the average length of rods in general use, and I cannot understand why. Anyone in doubt should try punching 16 yards of DT #8 medium-sinking line into a strong breeze or 18 yards of DT #8 floating line into 'dead-air' with suitable 9-foot and 10-foot rods. He will quickly notice how much easier and better his casting is with the shorter rod! The main reason for using a rod longer than 9 feet should be line control and lifting purposes.

My tournament fly-casting rods are made of carbon-fibre, and when something better comes along I shall consider it for my fishing rods. If carbon is good enough for ultimate performance, it is bound to be good enough for ordinary use, so why pay more for a material that may seem exotic but is not perceptibly better in use? The average caster uses no more than 60 per cent of the potential of a good rod, and I rather suspect that we are approaching the irreducible minimum in terms of wall thickness and diameter of

159

rods. No doubt further improvements will be made, but durability has to be a major consideration. Normal wear and tear must be accommodated without damage.

Oxide-lined rod rings should be standard throughout, since plastic-covered fly-lines shoot so much better through them than through other types. Butt- and tip-rings should have double legs, the remainder single legs. Anyone thinking of using snake-rings should examine the rod I used to use for casting demonstrations, on which the various lines and backings cut right through the varnish and whippings in places. The problem disappeared once I started using oxide-lined rings. Incidentally, only the whippings should be varnished with modern high-built epoxy material. The old practice, used even on expensive rods today, of spraying two thin coats over the rod blank and the whippings, has a very poor working life.

A screw-grip reel fitting is essential, because a sliding fitting can easily work loose. If you use a rod with a sliding fitting, hold it in place with waterproof tape.

The method of testing for the correct stiffness of a 9-foot #8 rod is described on page 29. Other rods mentioned, all made from carbon-fibre with middle-to-tip actions, have the following uses and features.

9-foot #6 – for delicate nymph fishing on small waters (*page 106*).

9-foot #7 – for nymph fishing on medium and large waters, and general-purpose fishing on small waters. Also ideal for a lady or young angler (*pages 136, 141*).

9-foot #8 – the ideal general-purpose rod (*described fully on pages 28 to 30. See also pages 36, 102, 109, 113, 116, 125, 141, 149, 156, 159*).

9-foot #9 – a powerful rod for increased casting distance and dealing with rough conditions (*page 150*).

9½-foot #7 – for nymph fishing on all waters where a longer line has to be lifted off the water and cast to another rising fish; also for lifting and controlling the line in boat-fishing (*page 136*).

9½-foot #8 – for nymph fishing from the bank on large waters; also for lifting and controlling the line in boat-fishing (*pages 109, 113*).

9½-foot #10 – for casting and lifting sinking lines in boat-fishing, and for fishing large flies in deep water (*page 125*).

9½ #13 – for casting and lifting very heavy sinking lines in boat-fishing, and for fishing very large flies in extremely deep water (*pages 125, 153*).

11-foot #6 – with 3-inch extension handle behind the reel fitting – for loch-style fishing from a boat (*pages 121, 145*).

15½-foot telescopic dapping rod – used because the extra length makes the blowline work properly from boats (*page 146*).

REELS AND BACKING LINES

THE REEL DESCRIBED on page 31, with a diameter of 3⅝ inches over the exposed rim and an inside width of ²⁹⁄₃₂ inch, is the smallest that will accept a DT #8 floating line together with a sensible reserve of backing. These capacities are: 55 yards of 25-pound braided Dacron (BD25); 45 yards of 20-pound hollow-weave Terylene (HWT20); and 50 yards of 20-pound hollow braided nylon (HBN20). 20-pound nylon mono can be used to increase the reserve, but it is more springy and may coil badly on the small-diameter spool. This reel will also accept: DT #8 neutral-density and 60 yards of HWT20 or 65 yards of HBN20; DT #8 medium-sink and 65 yards of HWT20 or 70 yards of HBN20; DT #8 extra-fast-sink and 95 yards of HWT20 or 85 yards of 25-pound hollow braided nylon (HBN25); WF #8 floating and 60 yards of HWT20 or 65 yards of HBN20; ST #8 floating and 90 yards of HBN25; ST #8 medium-sink and 95 yards of HBN25; and ST lead-core and 175 yards of 30-pound nylon monofilament.

Reels

The smallest reel I normally use is one of 3½ inches diameter over the exposed rim with an inside width of ¹³⁄₁₆ inch in conjunction with the following lines: DT #6 floating and 55 yards of BD25, 45 yards of HWT20 or 50 yards of HBN20; WF #8 floating and 40 yards of BD25; DT #8 medium-sink and backing as DT #6 above; ST #8 floating and 80 yards of HBN25; and ST #8 medium-sink and 85 yards of HBN25. It will not accept DT #7 floating or neutral-density lines together with adequate backing. I give this information in detail because my ideas about reel capacity seem to vary considerably from those claimed in the descriptive literature accompanying the various reels I have been asked to fill with lines and backing. It pays to take a cautious view when purchasing!

Multiplying reels, which use gearing to give a fast line recovery, can be useful, but they lack what might be described as 'feel' when a fish is being played and they are usually heavier and more expensive than single-action models. For much the same reasons I do not care for automatic reels, operated by clockwork springs. But it all boils down to personal preference.

Backing lines

Braided Dacron is the thinnest braided backing material available if breaking strains are compared. It can be joined to fly-lines very well with whipped loops, but it is expensive. 20-pound hollow braided nylon is slightly larger in diameter, but it is not large enough to make a Superglue splice over the line, so loops must be made with it. 20-pound hollow-weave Terylene is also slightly larger in diameter, but it can be spliced over the line or looped. 25-pound hollow braided nylon is again of increased diameter, but can be spliced or looped.

Nylon monofilament of round or oval section is very good for long casts with shooting-head lines, particularly with the short lead-core types with which frequent braking of the backing is necessary. However, it is prone to tangling by wind and coiling from being wound on a reel, although coils can be removed to some extent by stretching it thoroughly before use. Hollow braided nylon is the most user-friendly material for a shooting-head backing, but twists and tends to tangle if you brake persistently or let it run through your hand during line-shooting.

Spare reel spools are useful and economical when you start to accumulate the inevitable selection of lines. These spools can be kept in small purpose-made pouches or cases. However, each spool should have a self-adhesive label attached to face the backplate of the reel and indicating the line's AFTM number, type and shooting-head or weight-forward head length. A laundry marker pen is ideal for the purpose.

The reels and backing I normally take to a fishery are listed below, together with an indication of the lines I use with them. Of course, some are left in the car to lighten my fishing bag. The 30-pound BS nylon mono is knotted to the lead-core line loops, whereas the other backings have whipped loops for line attachment.

Size – 3⅝ inches diameter and 29/32 inch inside width

Reel and 50 yards of HBN20 for DT #8 floating or neutral-density lines.

Reel and 65 yards of HBN20 for WF #8 floating or neutral-density lines.

Spool and 65 yards of HBN20 for DT #7 floating or neutral-density and DT #8 medium-sink lines.

Spool and 90 yards of HBN25 for any shooting-head or dapping line.

Two spools and 170 yards of 30-pound nylon mono for any lead-core shooting-head.

Size – 3½ inches diameter and ¹³⁄₁₆ inch inside width

Two reels and 50 yards of HBN20 for DT #6 floating or neutral-density and DT #8 medium-sink lines.

Two spools and 80 yards of HBN25 for any shooting-head up to #9 and 39 feet long.

FLY-LINES

THE USES FOR the various types of fly-line are described from page 33 and in the various chapters on fishing. When you choose a line, pay particular attention to the surface finish. It should be smooth and firm to the touch, without any suggestion of tackiness. Some lines have an almost imperceptible surface film which tends to spoil shooting distance and double-haul performance.

Much ink has been used in discussing the merits or otherwise of dark- and light-coloured floating lines. Some argue that a dark-brown or black line does not flash in the air, whereas a light one does, so frightening the trout. My philosophy is that if I cannot see the fish, but it is close to where I am casting, it is more likely to be frightened by the fall of the line than by its flash, and the disturbance is unavoidable. However, if I can see the trout, then I try to place only the fly and leader in front of it, so line colour is immaterial.

Floating-line colours are, in my opinion, much more important in stillwater fly-fishing, when their visibility to the angler has to be considered. If the line is being watched for an indication of an offer, or being used as a range-finder before being lifted off before a cast is made to another rising fish, then visibility is crucial. In my experience pale colours, such as peach or tan, tend to merge into the reflective surface of the water. Chocolate brown and black lines appear as light grey and tend also to merge. Bright orange and brilliant white are good against a dark reflection, but fluorescent light green and yellow seem best, with green having the edge.

Provided they have looped backing ends, spare lines can be kept on the plastic spools on which they are supplied, ready to be interchanged when needed. An elastic band around the spool centre can be used to trap the leader or line end, and then the line can be wound on with the help of a pencil through the central hole as a spindle. A wide rubber band placed radially across and around the spool will stop line coming off, or the spool coming apart. *All spools must be labelled.*

The lines I have mentioned, together with their uses, are:

DT 6 floating – for accurate and delicate casting and for casting into light breezes and 'dead-air' conditions (*pages 106, 121, 141, 145*).

DT 7 floating – as above at longer range (*pages 136, 141*).

DT 8 floating – as above at even longer range (*page 37*).

WF 7 floating 40-foot head – for casting good distances delicately across light breezes or with the wind, when fishing with small flies (*page 136*)

WF 8 floating 40-foot head – as above, but for casting longer distances with larger flies (*pages 109, 113, 116*).

WF 8 floating 33-foot head – as above, but for beginners (*pages 58, 61, 77*).

WF 8 neutral-density 38-foot head – as WF 8 float, but to meet very slow-sinking needs (*page 149*).

DT 8 medium-sink – for casting into wind and learning to cast (*pages 36, 61*).

ST 8 floating 36 feet long – for casting distances up to 35 yards across or with the wind (*pages 50, 117, 125*).

ST 8 neutral-density 36 feet and 38 feet long – as ST 8 float above, but to meet very slow-sinking needs (*pages 109, 113, 156*).

ST 8 medium-sink 30 feet long – for casting distances up to 30 yards and for depths up to 10 feet, across or with the wind. Also for beginners to learn with and where the back-cast is restricted (*pages 37, 61, 73*).

ST 8 fast-sink 30 feet long – as ST 8 medium-sink above, but for depths up to 20 feet (*page 61*).

ST 8 fast-sink 38 feet long – for casting distances up to 40 yards, for depths up to 20 feet (*page 49*).

ST 9 medium-sink 39 feet long – for casting distances up to 40 yards and for depths up to 12 feet, across or with the wind (*page 150*).

ST 9 extra-fast-sink 30 feet or 33 feet long – for casting distances up to 30 yards and for depths up to 25 feet across or with the wind (*pages 102, 125*).

ST 11 extra-fast-sink 30 feet long – for casting distances up to 35 yards and for depths up to 35 feet across or with the wind (*page 125*).

ST 12 extra-fast-sink 36 feet long – for casting distances up to 45 yards and for depths up to 40 feet across or with the wind (*page 153*).

ST 375-grain lead-core 30 feet long – for casting distances up to 40 yards and for depths up to 50 feet (*pages 125, 153*).

ST 450-grain lead-core 30 feet long – as above, but with a faster sinking rate (*pages 125, 153*).

ST 550-grain lead-core 30 feet long – as above, but with a faster sinking rate (*pages 125, 153*).

Dapping blowline (medium), 15 yards (*page 146*).

All lines are looped with a 5⁄16 inch loop at the backing end and a 1⁄8 inch loop at the leader end.

—— *LINE-TRAYS AND LINE RAFTS* ——

THE LINE-TRAY is an important piece of equipment under certain circumstances, particularly if the weather is windy and/or you need to retrieve more quickly than the 'figure-of-eight' permits. A line-tray can be useful even in a boat if backing is being blown about and tangling, or the bottom boards have snags. Probably the best design is a tapered canvas pouch, with a wide, stiffened rim and a small drain-hole in the bottom. The tray-type with a canvas bottom is also satisfactory, provided it is 6 inches deep, but a netting bottom can bring problems if the wind causes an updraught through the netting, which, in turn, causes tangling.

Line rafts that float on the water can be useful if you always wade in nearly to the top of your waders, which is where the raft will float. However, if you are only knee-deep, a breeze may make line placement difficult because of the height difference. The standard type of line raft, with an inflated tubular periphery, is unsatisfactory in wind because the line is blown off too easily.

LEADERS

'LEADER' IS a comparatively modern term. The old name for this item was 'a cast', but this could be confused with the act of casting. It is better to eliminate such anomalies and, after all, a nylon leader does lead the line. A leader provides an inconspicuous link between the line and fly, and this is best achieved with a material that has little colour and is absolutely glint-free.

Many misconceptions arise about the use of different types of leader, so it is probably better to analyse the need rather than specify particular leaders. The following examples by no means cover every situation, but they are sufficient to give a broad understanding of the factors to be considered.

Leaders for the floating line

Floating lines are normally used in reasonably good conditions, or with the wind behind. This is because a strong side-wind sets up an uncontrollable drag on the fly, and the comparatively large diameter of a floating line makes it difficult to cast into a wind. I have already described the need to present the fly delicately and accurately to rising fish (*page 131*), and the DT line is well suited to this at ranges up to 20 yards. Beyond this, however, casting accuracy is not good enough even for an expert, and it is also difficult to see when the fly is taken.

The DT line casts more accurately than any other, and its tapered end dissipates the energy ensuring that the line straightens without splashing. The logical extension is a tapered leader. (By the way, no tournament accuracy caster would dream of using anything other than a specially knotted, steeply tapered nylon mono leader!) Line and leader will be on, or very close, to the surface, and freedom from knots is desirable to minimise disturbance, so a continuously tapered mono leader is what is needed. Different makes have different lengths and breaking strains, but from any of them you will be able to cut suitable 9-foot leaders tapering from 15 pounds to 7 pounds or from 10 pounds to 5 pounds. A 7-pound point will be necessary where large fish are present or size 8 flies and/or a DT 8 floating line are used. A 5-pound point can be used with size 10 flies or smaller and a DT 6 floating line fished on small waters, provided care is taken in playing fish.

The continuously tapered leader is also helpful in casting into dead-air or a very light breeze. Some advantage in straightening is gained in 'fishing the water' near the surface at long range, although you may need to brake the final shoot to help the leader to turn over. In this case a 9-foot continuous taper from 18 pounds down to 9 pounds could be used with, say, a 3-foot 7-pound point added with a 5-inch dropper at the knot. Whilst a nylon leader does not have the same weight as the end of the line, to create uniform energy transfer, it does have an inherent stiffness which is quite pronounced in continuous tapered makes and which assists turn-over.

While the new, braided nylon tapered leaders perform well, they are much larger in diameter than mono, which makes them more visible to the fish and that, I feel, is undesirable. I also have reservations about the overfit and sleeve attachment to the line, having seen the plastic coating, and therefore the leader, slip off a line. A friend hasn't used them since a trout he had hooked ran through weed and somehow rolled the sleeve off the leader and on to the line, again freeing the leader.

Conditions are bound to be relatively calm when you are casting a weighted nymph to relatively static trout that are deep and visible, so accuracy and depth of presentation are important. However, if you are to spot offers instantly, the sinking rate of the leader must be constant, and this can be achieved satisfactorily only using uniformly thick nylon mono, without knots. Leader length should vary from 12 to 16 feet, depending on the depth of the water, with a breaking strain of 6 pounds for flies up to size 12. Casts to individual cruising fish should not be more than, say, 14 yards or to a depth greater than 5 feet, otherwise the variables of casting accuracy and judgement of depth cannot be controlled. A 10-foot 7-pound leader and a size 8 heavily weighted nymph are needed to make the most of the situation.

If you are fishing deeply and slowly with the wind behind, you can use a 16-foot leader tapered continuously from 15 to 5 pounds with size 12 flies or smaller to assist straightening. But the fly has to be weighted to maintain its depth, because the retrieve exerts water pressure under the thick end of the leader, causing an unweighted fly to be lifted up. This lifting effect can be reduced by using 16 feet of 6-pound nylon mono (which is much thinner) near the line, or you might like to experiment with a double-tapered leader. One construction, starting from the line, is: 8 ft of 6 lb, 6 in of 9 lb, 6 in of 12 lb, 4 ft of 15 lb, 6 in of 12 lb, 6 in of 9 lb, 2 ft 6 in of 6 lb. The idea is that the thin leader near the line does not lift the heavier central part. Any number of permutations can be developed from this basic scheme.

I prefer to knot leaders to a loop whipped at the end of the line, which makes leader-changing a simple matter. The method is particularly relevant for tapered nylon, because it provides a reasonably smooth blend between line and leader, minimising the effect of the unavoidably larger knot.

Leaders for use with various floating lines and for dapping have been described in preceding chapters. They are:

9 ft long – 3 ft each of 15, 10, 7 lb nylon for bank-fishing and casting to rising fish (*page 37*).

10 ft long – continuously tapered to 6 lb nylon for bank-fishing at long range (*page 50*).

16 ft long – 6 lb, for bank-fishing with a weighted nymph (*page 106*).

12 ft long – 9 ft 6 in and a 4 in dropper of 7 lb, 3 ft 6 in point of 6 lb, for bank-fishing near the surface (*pages 109, 113*).

14 ft long – 11 ft and a 4 in dropper, 3 ft point, all of 7 lb, for boat-fishing very near the surface (*page 116*).

14 ft long – as above, but 9 lb (*page 117*).

13 ft 6 in long – 6 ft 6 in and a 5 in dropper, 3 ft 6 in and a 5 in dropper, 3 ft 6 in point, all of 6 lb, for boat-fishing, loch-style (*page 121*).

12 ft 6 in long – 9 ft 6 in and a 4 in dropper of 6 lb, 3 ft point of 5 lb, for bank-fishing during the evening rise (*page 136*).

9 ft long – 7 lb, for bank-fishing when nearly dark (*page 136*).

12 ft long – 9 ft and a 4 in dropper, 3 ft point, all of 7½ lb, for bank-fishing during the evening rise (*page 141*).

3 ft 6 in long – 10 lb, for dapping from a boat (*page 146*).

Leaders for the sinking line

The length and strength of leaders for sinking-line fishing vary according to the method used.

When flies or lures of size 6 or larger are fished at long range with WF or ST lines, the wind is normally behind, or at least helpful to, the caster. The leader tends to be blown straight or to the side of the line, which reduces the risk of tangles. Also, the line nearly always sinks faster than the leader and fly, so, whether or not the leader has straightened the line pulls downwards, again with a straightening effect. A weighted fly or lure may sink faster than the line, so the leader will sink with a humped profile. It is plain from this that a tapered leader isn't of much help, because the nylon is not stiff enough to deal with the weight of the fly, and any straightening above the water is achieved largely with help from the wind. Furthermore, if the water is reasonably deep, line- and fly-sinking rates take charge of the leader, whether or not it is straight to start with. It is clear, therefore, that a length of nylon mono will suffice and that (setting aside the size of the fish present and the drowning effect of the line) leader strength should be governed by the size of the fly or lure in use. As a general guide a 4-inch lure needs 15-pound nylon; a 3-inch, 12-pound; a 2-inch, 10-pound; and a size 6, 8-pound to minimise the risk of 'cracking off' in casting. In very clear water, a leader length of 15 feet is needed for boat- fishing, but 12 feet is satisfactory when the water carries some colour. These lengths can usually be reduced to 12 feet and 9 feet for bank-fishing because the fish do not have such a 'global' view of the fly as they do in deep water, where they can see the line clearly from below.   ·

A plain mono leader is adequate, too, at shorter ranges with slow-sinking DT or WF lines cast across or with the wind. Size 6 flies need 8-pound; size 8, 7-pound; and size 10 or smaller, 6-pound.

The average angler will need all the help available when he is casting into a strong wind, and he will get it from a steeply tapered leader used in conjunction with a DT line to achieve the best straightening effect. The water will be rough, so a 7-foot leader will be adequate, and a few knots, together with a strong point, will pass unnoticed by the trout. A suitable taper can be made from 1 foot 9 inches each of 20-pound, 15-pound, 10-pound and 7-pound nylon. The same strengths can be used for casting into 'dead-air', but in lengths of 2 feet 3 inches or, better still, a continuous taper.

Leaders suggested for use with the various sinking lines described in preceding chapters are:

6 ft long – 8 lb b/s for bank-fishing and casting into wind (*page 36*).

9 ft long – 7 lb b/s for bank-fishing at medium and long range (*pages 49, 102, 109, 113*).

15 ft long – 8 lb b/s for boat-fishing at medium range (*page 125*).

15 ft long – 10 lb b/s for boat-fishing at medium range (*page 125*).

12 ft long – 7 lb b/s for bank-fishing at medium range (*page 149*).

12 ft long – 8 lb b/s for bank-fishing at long range (*page 150*).

12 ft long – 10 lb b/s for boat-fishing at long range (*page 154*).

10 ft long – 7½ lb b/s for bank-fishing at medium range (*page 157*).

FLIES

FISHING IS the only sport in which the prey catches the sportsman, or rather, his flies! This may sound dramatic, but it is a fact that the fish we catch have been persuaded to take a fly, though it is often difficult to say why. So, to a considerable extent, we use flies which experience or recommendation tells us are taken in the conditions prevailing.

Having read the chapters describing fishing days, you will have a fairly clear idea of what flies have been successful at different times of the season in my experience, and that the marrow spoon has yielded, or not, a great deal of information about the trout's food intake. Scanning the descriptions of fish captures in which the food intake was known, and relating the type of fly used – poor food imitation or semi-food imitation – to the food found in the trout, we find:

Poor food imitation	*Food in trout*
Black Chenille	none
Black Chenille	snails and caddis larvae
Orange Chenille	none
Orange Chenille	caddis larvae
Black Tadpole	none
Yellow Tadpole	none
Orange Tadpole	daphnia
White Tadpole	daphnia and midge pupae
Pink Tadpole	midge pupae
Grey Muddler Minnow	none

Grey Muddler Minnow	daphnia
Grey Muddler Minnow	snails
Grey Muddler Minnow	snails and bloodworms

Semi-food imitation	*Food in trout*
Cove's Pheasant Tail	midge pupae
Cove's Pheasant Tail	daphnia and midge pupae
Cove's Pheasant Tail	bloodworms and midge pupae
Olive Midge Pupae	daphnia and midge pupae
Olive Midge Pupae	bloodworms and midge pupae
Olive Midge Pupae	daphnia
Iven's Green Nymph	fry
Invicta	midge pupae
Mallard and Claret	midge pupae
Mallard and Claret	none
Soldier Palmer	midge pupae
Black Zulu	daphnia
Gold-ribbed Hare's Ear	dahpnia and midge pupae
Silver Invicta	fry
White Muddler Minnow	fry

From this it might reasonably be deduced that:

- Trout that have not been feeding will sometimes take a semi-food imitation, but are more likely to succumb to something large, lively and/or brightly coloured.

- There are occasions when a well-presented semi-imitation will attract trout feeding on the one food form being imitated.

- There are many occasions when trout are feeding on two food forms and will take a semi-imitation of one of them.

- Trout will often change from one or even two food forms to take a fly which could not be regarded as a semi-imitation of either.

The fishing situations I have described are intended as a guide to method options, not to trout food, but they do tell a story! However, if I were asked to place the stomach contents of the trout I catch in descending order of importance, it would probably be: midge pupae, daphnia, nothing, fry, caddis larvae, snails, caddis pupae, bloodworms. Given time to fish more waters, I would expect to see included also: damselfly and pond olive nymphs, lesser water boatmen, and shrimps.

To say that artificial flies for stillwater fly-fishing are numerous is an understatement! A magnificent book listing 600 patterns was published recently, and previously I had been fascinated by another book listing more than 100 patterns. However, for purely practical reasons, the contents of our fly-boxes have to be restricted to a sensible but limited selection, and the best way to make that selection is to examine the trout's taking and feeding potential at intervals throughout the season and choose flies to suit.

Early season flies

With the water cold following winter, any small food forms are confined to deep water, and largely on or near the bottom. Weed growth is minimal, so there is negligible protection for them, but most insects are in their larval state, hidden in burrows, whereas snails and caddis (sedge) larvae, which live on the bottom, are at greater risk of being eaten. With few if any suspended life forms, the water is clear and the light penetrating, so underwater visibility is very good.

The proportion of recently stocked trout is at its greatest at this time of the season, and their period of acclimatisation to natural feeding is extended because of the small amount of food available. Some trout start to take a few snails and caddis larvae, but bottom-feeding is alien to them. Food was plentiful during their time in the rearing cages or hatchery and was taken near the surface. However, significant numbers of trout are willing to sample various flies, provided they are presented in an attractive manner. These trout are often in shoals, which, considering they have lived their lives in a close-knit rearing community, is only natural. The first priority, then, is to locate a shoal, and then to present a fly which triggers a positive response.

Trout have good eyesight, and recent experiments suggest that they have colour vision, particularly in the red zone, good perception of contrasts, and an inability to limit the amount of light entering the eye.

With the water sufficiently calm and clear for me to see the fish, which is relatively unusual in lakes and reservoirs, I would have no hesitation in using the following semi-imitations:
- Size 12 Olive Midge Pupa or Cove's Pheasant Tail for midge pupae

- Size 12 Black and Peacock Spider for snails
- Size 12 long-shank Stick Fly for caddis larvae.

All would have a small amount of copper wire wound under the dressing to make them sink quickly and would be retrieved very slowly, near the trout, on a long leader. I would watch the leader carefully while the fly is sinking and during the retrieve, as takes are often extremely gentle. In some trout lakes, especially in the South of England, the water is permanently clear, so this is the standard method of fishing.

Later it will be very much a matter of casting to individual fish, and if the water is deep, quite a lot of copper wire will be needed under the dressing to get the fly down to the trout before it moves away. As to patterns, I would be content with a size 12 Shrimp or a size 10 Damselfly Nymph. A killing method is to let the fly sink in front of the fish and then draw it gently away at the last moment.

When the water is deep and the trout can't be seen, it is a question of 'fishing the water' to find a shoal and thoroughly searching the depths within casting range. Proper account must be taken of light intensity in relation to the likely depth of the fish. A trout sees a fly fishing above it as a silhouette against the bright sky whatever the fly's colour, so it makes sense to use a black fly to enhance the contrast. This is seen in clear contrast, too, against a backdrop of water when viewed straight ahead, but much less distinctly against a dark bottom. A white fly also appears dark from below, in mild contrast ahead, and in full contrast against a dark bottom.

Fly movement caused by the retrieve is important if an impression of life, and therefore food, is to be conveyed to the trout. If this can be enhanced by lively movement within the fly, so much the better. These two factors can be used to induce a fish to seize a fly before its fellows have a chance to catch it. This is when strong, powerful takes can be expected, particularly when the trout is moving away from the rod, so strong leaders are essential.

Movement within a fly can be created by incorporating a marabou tail or wing, or a soft hackle. A tail may bring a few abortive offers when it is nipped by the trout, but flies with tails seem to catch more fish than those without. For years my first choice was a size 8 Black Chenille, with a White Chenille of the same size in reserve. More recently, I have achieved even better results with a size 10 long-shank Black Tadpole, again with white as the alternative.

Given freedom of movement along the bank, the prolonged use

of these flies will do no harm, but if I were confined to one spot, I would use them only for short periods. Between times I would fish slowly and deeply with a size 12 long-shank Stick Fly on the point and a size 12 Olive Midge Pupa or Cove's Pheasant Tail on the dropper, all of them weighted. Although it may seem contradictory, weight in flies does add life to a very slow movement, especially to the dropper, where any pull on the leader causes the fly to lift, pause, and then sink again.

Flies for May and June

Given reasonable weather conditions, the water warms up in May and June, which brings a dramatic increase in available trout food. Snails and caddis larvae on the bottom are supplemented by midge larvae (bloodworms), which emerge from their burrows. Midges and sedges pupate, then hatch in increasing numbers. In fertile waters, daphnia multiply rapidly and drift on the surface or just below in dull weather, but sink to depths of 15 feet and more in bright conditions. Minute organisms proliferate in the water to the extent that clarity is considerably reduced, which doubtless makes the fish feel more secure, particularly in a good ripple, and they feed higher in the water.

The regular stocking which is now normal makes for a mixture of trout, from fully acclimatised to completely new stock. In fertile waters, acclimatised trout follow the clouds of daphnia and take such pupae as they come across or, in more leisurely mood, browse in the weed for snails, pupae or larvae. In less fertile waters, the trout tend to remain quiet, expending minimum energy, while waiting for a good hatch of insects on which to feed.

The pattern is much as before in clear-water lakes, except that they have more weed and greater numbers of the same food forms, together with mayflies in some of them.

Fertile waters

Trout location is as vital in fertile lakes as elsewhere, but the opportunity and the choice of flies, are much increased. A bank angler can position himself where a wind drift brings daphnia feeders through an area. If the weather is not bright, their feeding depths will vary from 1 to 3 feet, and midge pupae will usually be taken as well. Where the objective is to 'jolt' the trout away from daphnia, or to interest recently stocked fish, I have every confidence in a size 10 long-shank Tadpole. Black should be the first choice, with white and orange as alternatives. Orange is particularly effective when the sun comes out briefly! Viva and Whisky flies are also good, but do not possess the same movement within the fly. A more imitative approach can be made by fishing a size 10 long-shank Cove's Pheasant Tail on the point and a weighted size 12 Olive Midge Pupa on the dropper. Alternatively, a size 10 long-shank Stick Fly can be used on the point. Trout browsing on or near the bottom are better fished for with the same flies, but slowly and deeply on a floating line and a very long leader.

Daytime boat-fishing can be interesting at this time of season, and the freedom of movement that it gives means that it is a good way of finding fish. Grey Muddler Minnows fished on the point and dropper are successful when fished from an anchored boat, and Mallard and Claret, Soldier Palmer and Black Zulu (all size 12) are good fished loch-style as a team of three. I would be happy with two size 10 Black Tadpoles or a team consisting of an Allrounder (on the point), Invicta and Red Palmer (again, all size 12) as alternatives.

Infertile waters

All that I have said about the use of Tadpoles applies when dealing with freshly stocked trout in infertile waters, though I would be inclined to use a colour not often seen by the trout, such as fluorescent pink, green, yellow or blue, where fishing pressure is heavy. For the middle part of the day, when the fish are browsing, a good plan is to fish a size 12 Black and Peacock Spider on the point and a size 12 Cove's Pheasant Tail on the dropper. Alternatives are a size 12 Stick Fly and a size 12 Olive Midge Pupa. The boat-fisher can anchor in different places to try for large fish deep-down with a size 6 long-shank White Tadpole.

Sooner or later there is a nice rise to midges or sedges. A good combination then, from the bank, is a size 12 Invicta on the point and a size 12 Olive Sedge Pupa on the dropper, with a size 12 Wickham's Fancy and a size 14 long-shank Gold-ribbed Hare's Ear as alternatives. For boat-fishing, the loch-style teams of flies listed above are effective during a rise.

Clear waters

Longer periods of waiting for trout to come within casting range are likely as the season progresses, but a quick and delicate presentation is essential when they do. The system described on page 105 may be used, and frequently a Cove's Pheasant Tail, but size 12. A weighted size 10 Mayfly Nymph is a useful alternative.

Flies for July and August

Fertile and infertile waters

July and August are the months when we expect two major problems: hot weather and weed. These are of considerable concern to the bank angler, but they are less problematical for boat anglers on large, deep waters. However, specialised methods are needed to make the best of daytime fishing in both situations whereas early-morning and evening rises can be dealt with in standard fashion.

Boats are not usually available for early-morning fishing, so it makes good sense to consider bank-fishing first. Reasonable hatches of chironomids (midges) may come off early on, often in quite calm conditions, so a delicate approach is necessary. A size 12 Wickham's Fancy (point) and a size 14 Gold-ribbed Hare's Ear (dropper) work well, with similar sizes of Dunkeld and Olive Midge Pupa as alternatives. The leader should be left ungreased, and the depth of the flies controlled by the initial sinking time and the speed of retrieve. As standard practice, use the largest flies the trout will accept. Small hooks are made from fine wire, which carries a greater danger of their straightening or pulling out – something too awful to contemplate when it may be the fish of the season that escapes!

Daytime bank-fishing can be almost hopeless when it is really warm, but not quite! There's always dry fly! A double-taper #6 floating line and a 10-foot 5-pound leader is a good combination, with a size 14 Wickham's Fancy or Greenwell's Glory well treated with floatant, but the leader left ungreased. A degreased leader does not show up on the surface, but the best course of action is to fish with the line and most of the leader lying on the edge of a light weed- bed, with the fly over clear water. The advantages are that any air movement will not drift the line and leader, and that the leader will be rendered as inconspicuous as possible. The number of trout which patrol the edge of the weed during an afternoon can be surprising. If one does show interest in your fly, do nothing until you see the leader move, and then strike gently.

The best sport of all is to be expected during the evening rise (*page 131*). A size 12 Olive Midge Pupa on the point and a size 14

Gold-ribbed Hare's Ear on the dropper are good before the rise begins, with a size 12 Olive Sedge Pupa and a size 14 Cove's Pheasant Tail excellent alternatives. The important thing is to fish the flies at precisely the right depth. During the rise proper, I use hardly anything but a lightly dressed size 12 Wickham's Fancy or Invicta cast to individual rising fish. Every fisherman has his own favourites, and nothing can beat an accurate cast made by an angler with total confidence in the fly or flies he is using. A size 10 G&H Sedge can work well in the near darkness, especially when it is retrieved quickly on the surface. These comments on bank-fishing apply to most types of water.

Boat-fishing (*page 124*) can be particularly effective on large waters given wind and no prolonged heatwave. The heavy lines used allow large lures to be cast easily. Accordingly, heavily dressed size 6 long-shank Black or Orange Tadpoles can be used to good effect. Size and colour are important in making an impact on trout 20 feet or more deep in slightly coloured water.

But it's the boat angler fishing loch-style in the evening who has the best opportunities for sport on large waters. Casting 'teams of three' towards rising fish can be very rewarding, with size 12 Mallard and Claret (point), Soldier Palmer, Black Zulu, alternatively Allrounder (point), Invicta and Red Palmer all good. In late August a size 10 Daddy-long-legs is a useful dapping fly, but have at least six available as they quickly become waterlogged.

Clear waters

Nymph fishing can still be rewarding if it is not too hot, although both fish and insects are likely to be lethargic during the middle of the day. Moreover, the trout will have seen so many weighted nymphs plopping in that you'll need the stealth of a Red Indian at some fisheries. A method that works occasionally is to watch for a trout that patrols regularly and then cast a fly into its path and leave it on the bottom. As the trout returns, pull the nymph upward and it may very well be taken. The variables are difficult to control, but a success is memorable. A dry fly is always worth a try, too, but your patience will be tested!

Flies for autumn and winter

All waters

The new strains of rainbow trout may be caught in perfect condition long after the brown trout season is over. How long you fish on for is largely a matter of personal choice, but for me it is governed by temperature. Cold hands are also the signal for reduced trout feeding activity. That is not to say that a mild, late-autumn day at the waterside is not a pleasure. It is, but it is not always productive.

September often brings good daytime sport, with daphnia in decline and the trout feeding well on a variety of food forms, but with early-morning and late-evening activity diminishing progressively as temperatures begin to drop. It is a pleasant change not to have to get up early or stay out late, but it is also interesting that bank-fishing improves greatly and is often as good as it was early in the season, with the prospect of some large fish as well. Boat-fishing can also be excellent in September, and all the methods I have described can be employed to good effect, except that dapping tails off as the surface temperature falls. During October and beyond, feeding times are limited to warmer periods in the day, which may last only an hour or two, so mid-day breaks may have to be forgotten.

It has been said that September is good because the trout are feeding up for winter, but this is not really so. They are great conservers of energy and feed only when the food is sufficient to justify the effort needed. A well-fed hatchery-reared fish carries its rations on its back, so to speak, and it can live for a long time without feeding. It is unreasonable to expect it to rush about trying to find something to eat, but should some easy pickings become available, such as a hatch of chironomids, a shoal of fry or some daphnia, then that's another matter. So September trout may give the impression of being keen, but only because food is available, not for 'stocking up'.

Large waters see a significant movement of trout towards the banks at about the end of September. They feed as the opportunity arises, but sexual maturity and the search for suitable spawning facilities is the real motivation. Trout need running water and small gravel in which to spawn, and brown trout take advantage of any opportunity, even though it's provided by nothing more than a large ditch running into a water. Rainbows spawn without man's help in only a few places in this country, but strains which develop sexually are just as interested in finding suitable spawning places as are the browns. Any inflow of water is attractive to them, and these places sometimes produce good catches.

Reservoir towers and other prominent structures harbour large shoals of coarse-fish fry which are attractive to both browns and rainbows moving shorewards, resting in deep, relatively dark water between feeding spells.

Fisheries with seasons extending into October, or even winter, may have late additional stockings of rainbows which, because of the limited food supply, take longer than normal to acquire natural feeding habits. However, they occasionally show an interest in small lures and sport can be reasonably good, but only for short periods during the day. A more careful approach to the water is needed too, as water clarity improves progressively with the lower temperatures.

So, which flies should be used if a modicum of success is to be achieved? For bank-fishing on large waters a natural bank with a reasonably clear bottom, a nice ripple, and some small shoals of fry is a good location, and here a size 10 Grey Muddler Minnow may be successful when fished in relatively shallow water on a neutral-density line. This fly has a certain buoyancy which helps to keep it out of weed, thus avoiding a good deal of frustration. Trout caught may contain various food forms as well as fry. A size 12 Silver Invicta is also a good choice if fished slowly on a floating or neutral-density line. It seems to be taken as an insect or a small fry. These patterns may go on catching well into October in mild weather, with a size 10 White Tadpole and a size 12 Allrounder as substitutes.

Boat-fishing for fry-feeding trout lurking in deep water demands a large, light-coloured lure with plenty of life, and there's nothing better than a size 6 long-shank White Marabou Muddler Minnow.

A watch should always be kept for any evidence of chironomid hatches, when a size 12 Olive Midge Pupa or Cove's Pheasant Tail should produce results, particularly from the bank. Fish may also be bottom-feeding on snails, in which case a size 12 Black and Peacock Spider fished slowly close to the bottom may do the trick.

It is sound policy to remain mobile on small fisheries, especially if regular stockings are made. Mobility makes it easier to locate a shoal of fish, and when that's accomplished, nothing beats a size 10 Black Tadpole with White and Orange as alternatives. If you *are* confined to one spot, then a few casts from time to time may prove successful, but trout will soon be put off by continual casting. It is better to fish slowly with a floating line and a very long leader with lightly weighted flies, such as a size 12 Black and Peacock Spider on the point and a size 12 Silver Invicta on the dropper. Alternatives would be a size 10 Stick Fly (point) and a size 12 Gold-ribbed Hare's

Ear. In very cool water neither the fish nor the insects are in a great hurry to do anything, so it's a good idea to give the trout a chance to move into an area without disturbance, when it may sample your fly. Evidence of interest in hatching chironomids should be responded to immediately with the flies mentioned above being fished near the surface, since the activity may not last for long.

LANDING-NETS

A TRIANGULAR NET with arms at least 20 inches long and a net depth of 24 inches is adequate for most stillwater trout fishing, but one with 24-inch arms and a 30-inch net is advisable if double-figure trout are present.

Some of the many designs of folding net, with short telescopic handles and a belt-clip, are superb pieces of engineering and a joy to behold, but they do have disadvantages. Any mechanical device is subject to operating problems sooner or later, and one might crop up just as a specimen trout is ready for the net. Nets also become a little smelly after a number of trout have been landed, even though the mesh is well rinsed, and this smell is eventually transferred to your clothes, which may also become damp. However, if you stay in one spot on the bank, or fish from a boat, the net can be put down fully extended.

I take a simpler approach by using a screw-in triangular net head on a glass-fibre handle 45 inches long with a hard nylon cone glued in its end. Whipped to the handle 22 inches from the net head is a 2-inch loop made from ⅜-inch diameter braided nylon cord. A lanyard of the same material, 54 inches long with a 2-inch whipped loop at one end and burned to a point at the other (the hard end), is joined to the handle loop. I carry the net diagonally across my back, net down with the lanyard over my right shoulder and then brought down my front, past my left thigh, to be threaded through the net triangle next to the handle and tied with a half-bow knot, leaving a 6-inch spare end. If the hanging net tends to drag, it can be tied up by pushing the hard end of the lanyard through the triangle from the inside, out through the net rim. Pull up the net bottom and push the end of the lanyard through two or three meshes. Tie the bow again at the triangle. The net is then tied up nicely out of harm's way. When the hard end is pulled the bow comes undone and the net is released ready for use.

The net head tends to keep away from my clothing and is more comfortable than a 'folder'. When I'm wading, I can push the end with the nylon cone into the bottom ready for immediate use, though I remove the lanyard. I also use the net as a temporary line-tray by pushing it in the bottom at an angle in front and draping the net over the triangle to form a shallow bag. Where long leaders are used regularly, or you are fishing a dam wall in rough weather, the same system can be used, but incorporate an extension handle which provides a much longer 'reach'.

One snag with landing-nets is they do provide many snags on which hooks are easily caught up, either when a hook falls out of a fish in the net or when more than one fly is being used. I've even seen a dropper hook in the net rim as an angler has tried to net a trout hooked on the point fly – and the fish was lost. Time wasted in untangling hooks or repairing leaders during the precious minutes of an evening rise is a great loss, so I then beach my fish whenever possible (*page 157*).

—— *FISHING BAG AND CONTENTS* ——

I LIKE TO travel light when I'm actually fishing, so I keep all my tackle, except nets and rods, in a canvas holdall in the boot of my car and transfer only a minimum amount to my fishing bag. But any fishing bag should be large enough to hold two or three trout in a thick polythene bag and a spare reel spool as well as the items listed below. Mine is 18 × 12 × 6 inches and is made of strong waterproof canvas. It has two large pockets on its front and a thick adjustable canvas strap 2½ inches wide. It always contains:

Three foam-lined fly-boxes	Spring balance
Small hook-sharpening stone	Tin of detergent powder
Tin of Red Mucilin floatant	Polythene bag for fish
A torch	Plastic box holding four spools
A small tin holding my rod	of nylon leader material
licence, fishing permit and	Marrow spoon
two sticking plasters	Pencil
Polaroid sunglasses	Priest
Scissors	Small towel

—— BOAT-FISHING EQUIPMENT ——

MY STANDARD boat-fishing equipment consists of a 4-inch or 6-inch G-clamp with cord attached, a 4-foot square drogue, and a buoyancy waistcoat. More specialised gear is a padded plank seat, a 60-foot length of rope, an additional G-clamp and cord, an anchor and rope, and two more drogues 3 feet and 5 feet square.

—— CONCLUSION ——

THE DETAIL I have given on the subject of tackle is to guide the angler who is considering relatively specialised methods of fishing. However, there are ways and means of experimenting without going to the trouble and expense of buying a number of rods and their associated reels and lines.

Once you have become a good caster, you will find you are able to make a few compromises, and that you can try all the methods described with a surprisingly small amount of tackle. You may not achieve optimum performance, but you will certainly be in with a chance. This is what you will need:

9-foot #8 carbon rod.

Reel $3\frac{5}{8}$ inches in diameter and $\frac{29}{32}$ inches wide with 60 yards of 20-pound hollow braided nylon backing with a looped end for WF and DT lines.

Spare spool with 90 yards of 25-pound hollow braided nylon backing for shooting-heads.

Spare spool with 170 yards of 30-pound nylon mono for shooting-heads.

DT #8 medium-sinking line for casting into wind.

DT #7 floating line for delicate casting to rising fish.

WF #8 floating line with a 40-foot head for long-range fishing near the surface.

WF #8 neutral-density line with a 36-foot head for fishing up to, say, 5 feet deep.

ST #8 medium-sinking line 33 feet long for fishing up to, say, 10 feet deep.

ST #9 extra-fast-sinking line 33 feet long for fishing up to, say, 30 feet deep.

15 yards of medium dapping blowline.

All lines should be looped at both ends.

Spools of 15-pound, 10-pound, 8-pound, 7-pound and 6-pound nylon monofilament for leaders.

Flies will be covered by the following basic selection. The numbers refer to size and LS= long-shank.

Olive Midge Pupa, size 12 and 12, weighted
Cove's Pheasant Tail, 12
Black and Peacock Spider, 12
Stick Fly, 12
Soldier Palmer, 12
Invicta, 12 and 14
G&H Sedge, 10
Gold-ribbed Hare's Ear, 12 and 14, weighted
Daddy-long-legs, 10
Allrounder, 12
Shrimp, 12, weighted

Grey Muddler Minnow, 8LS
Black Marabou Tadpole, 6LS
White Marabou Tadpole, 6LS
Orange Marabou Tadpole, 6LS
Mallard and Claret, 12
Black Zulu, 12
Silver Invicta, 12
Wickham's Fancy, 12 and 14
Greenwell's Glory, 14
Mayfly Nymph, 10LS, weighted
Damselfly Nymph, 12, weighted

The other gear you will need is a line-tray, a landing-net, a bag and standard contents (but only one fly-box) (*see page 181*), and a 4-foot square drogue.

Detailed analysis will show that the types of line and leader and the fly sizes do not always match those mentioned previously, but they are close enough to be effective. Furthermore, as any experienced angler will confirm, this number of items is by no means large when compared with those normally acquired over a year or two. The main thing is that you should have lots of fun with your experiments, tight lines, long casts and heavy creels, and that real pleasure that I sometimes think only fishermen know.

Glossary

Ace of Spades – A black fly made with feathers and chenille.

AFTM number – The weight specification for the first 30 feet of fly-line, laid down by the Association of Fishing Tackle Manufacturers.

Air-resistance – Resistance to the front of the loop of line pushing into the air during the backward and forward casts.

Algal bloom – Large quantities of minute green and blue plants that appear in the water during warm weather.

Angle of cast – The angle made by the bottom of the line loop with the water or grass.

Aerialise (the line) – To cast a line into the air from the grass or water.

Backing – 50 yards or more of thin line knotted to the reel spool and joined to the fly-line, providing a reserve if a big fish runs a long way.

Back-cast – The act of casting a line behind you.

Belly – The thick part of a fly-line.

Blagdon – A large reservoir trout fishery near Bristol.

Bobbin-holder – A tool used in fly-tying to keep the silk under light tension.

Boron – A strong material used for making tubular fly-rods.

British Casting Association – The UK national organisation that makes rules for casting competitions, organises tournaments and ratifies records.

British trout distance record – The greatest distance achieved by a UK caster with a 3-metre maximum length rod and a 15-metre minimum length line weighing no more than 42 grammes.

Butt action (rod) – A fly-rod that bends all the way down to its handle when flexed during the casting of a fly-line.

Caddis larva – The popular name for the stage between egg and pupa in the development of a sedge fly.

Calm lane – A long, narrow area of calm water that divides two rippled areas.

Carbon – Often called graphite. A strong fibre material used for making tubular fly-rods.

Cast – The act of making a fly-line travel backwards or forwards and straighten in the air or on the water.

Cast-holder – The old name for a thin disc of material with notches around the periphery and fly clips on the face, and on which a spare leader was wound.

Casting along a wall – Pretending the rod-tip is travelling beside a high wall in casting to keep its movement straight.

Casting stroke – A backward or forward rod-movement in casting.

Chew – A large reservoir trout fishery near Bristol.

Chironomid pupa – The next stage of development after the larva and before the adult of the chironomid or midge family.

Creel – An old-fashioned fishing basket made of wickerwork.

Dacron – A thin braided backing material.

Dead-air – Still air conditions, usually with a damp atmosphere, in early morning or late evening.

Double-haul – Pulling the line downwards quickly with the left hand during the backward and forward strokes of a rod.

Double-taper – A fly-line tapered equally at each end of a central belly.

Drag – Unnatural movement of the fly caused by the action of wind or water on the line.

Drift (water) – The surface flow of the water caused by wind.

Drowning (line) – When the whole line is towed under by a fish.

Entomology – The study of insects.

Extension (line) – The straightening of a line behind or in front of the caster.

Figure-of-eight (retrieve) – A method of drawing in a fly-line during fishing and storing the retrieved line within the left hand.

Final forward delivery – The last forward cast that places a fly-line on the water.

Flick – The small, angular wrist movement at the end of the arm travel during casting which helps to make the line travel quickly.

Floatant – A dressing to make a line, backing, leader or fly float.

Floating line – A fly-line with air bubbles trapped in its plastic coating, or one which has been greased.

Fly – A hook with a fur and feather or other dressing designed to attract trout.

Fly-line – A modern plastic-covered line or traditional silk line.

Fly-tying – The act of making a fly.

Fly-tying silk – Thin thread, in many colours, supplied on a bobbin.

Fly-vice – A small vice having pointed jaws to hold a hook during fly-tying.

Forward cast – The act of making the line extend in front of a caster.

Forward-taper (line) – Otherwise called a weight-forward line. A line that has between 28 and 45 feet of heavy line continuously connected to thin shooting line.

Glass-fibre – A strong fibre material used for making tapered tubular fly-rods.

Greased – A line, backing, leader or fly dressed with floatant.

Grey Lure – An artificial fly on two hooks joined in tandem with long grey feathers attached.

Gunwale – The upper edge of a boat's side.

Handle – A shaped grip, usually made of cork, at the bottom of a rod.

Hand movement – The path the rod hand takes during casting.

Haul-down – The quick downward movement of the left hand during the double-haul.

Induced take – When a trout takes the fly after it sinks in front of it and is then drawn away.

Intermediate shoots – The line shoots made during the false casts before the final delivery.

Lead-core (line) – A heavy line loaded with metal in the centre of its braided core.

Leader – A length of nylon monofilament attached to the fishing end of the line and to which the fly is knotted.

Left-hand wind – Turning the reel with the left hand.

Limit – The maximum number of trout permitted to be taken during a specified period.

Line-core – The strong thread or braided material in the centre of a plastic-covered fly-line.

Line shortening – The act of pulling line in with the left hand.

Line-tray – A tray worn on a belt to hold retrieved line or backing.

Loop – The loop formed by a fly-line as it is extended backwards and forwards.

Middle/tip (rod action) – A fly-rod that bends from the tip down to the middle during casting.

Mixed limit – Mixed usually refers to brown and rainbow trout. See 'Limit' above.

Narrow loop – A small separation between the top and bottom of the loop.

Needle-knot – A special knot for joining leaders or backing to a fly-line.

Neutral-density (line) – A plastic-coated line that sinks very slowly.

No 3 line – A braided and oil-dressed silk line equivalent to AFTM #6.

Nylon mono – Abbreviation of nylon monofilament – used for leaders or backing.

Nymphing (trout) – Feeding trout eating the nymphs or pupae of insects just below or at the surface. Nymphing also refers to the method of fishing artificial nymphs.

Nymphs – The stage between egg and adult of upwinged flies. Pupa imitations.

Offer – When a trout attempts to take an artificial fly being fished.

Overhand knot – The simplest knot formed by 'one turn and back through the hole'.

Overhang – The short length of backing between rod-tip and shooting-head.

Oxide rod rings – Steel-framed rod rings with polished aluminium-oxide linings.

Parachute cast – A method of casting which places a fly-line gently on the water.

Plastic-coated line – A modern fly-line made with a metal-powder-impregnated plastic-coating on braided (or similar) core.

Point – The extreme end of the leader away from the line, sometimes called a tippet.

Ratchet check – A spring-controlled 'click-drag' mechanism inside the reel.

Reel – The line winding and storing spool attached to the bottom of the rod.

Red Mucilin – A proprietary clear jelly floatant in a small red tin.

Refraction – The scientific term for the bending of light rays when they pass through the water surface.

Release – The act of letting go the line with the left hand so that it can shoot.

Retrieve – The pulling in of line with the left hand during fishing.

Rings – The round guides on the rod through which the line slides.

Ripples (in line) – Waviness in the top and bottom of the line loop.

Rise up – The act of the left hand rising up as the line straightens during the double-haul sequence.

Rod-drift – A little extra rod-tip movement during a cast, made after the 'flick' has taken place.

Salmonidae – The general term for gamefish embracing trout, sea-trout and salmon.

Sea-trout – A brown trout (*Salmo trutta*) that is hatched in a river, migrates to the sea to feed, and returns to breed.

Shooting – The action of line or backing moving through the rod rings during casting.

Shooting-taper – A shooting-head.

Shoulder twist (swing) – Rotation of the shoulders during casting as seen from above.

Silk line – A fly-line made from braided silk and dressed with linseed oil.

Sinking line – A fly-line that sinks.

Sink-tip – A floating line with a short length of integral sinking line at the fishing end.

Smash take – When a trout takes a fly violently and breaks the leader.

Snake-ring – A rod ring made of wire bent into an open coil form.

Splice – A method of joining two sections of line, or line to backing.

Split-cane rod – A fly-rod constructed of six long triangular section strips of cane, glued together to form a larger hexagonal section.

Stock-fish (stockie) – Trout newly introduced to the water.

Strike – Lifting, swinging or pulling the rod quickly to hook a fish.

Surface tension (surface film) – The 'skin' formed on the surface of the water, which varies with atmospheric pressure and other factors. It is most clearly demonstrated by the curve on the surface of water in a glass.

Tackle – General fishing equipment.

Takes – The same as offers.

Tearing off – Pulling a fly-line off the water immediately into the back-cast.

Terrestrial (insect) – Insects blown from the land on to water.

Viva – A black artificial fly with a green fluorescent tail.

Vinyl coat – A liquid plastic which is applied to whippings and which remains flexible when dry.

Wading – When an angler wades into the water to fish, usually wearing thigh or breast waders (where permitted) to keep dry.

Weight-forward line – As forward-taper line.

Whipping silk – Fine thread wound over a join between two lines in a close spiral, or to bind on rod rings.

Wide loop – Opposite to narrow loop.

Wire rings – Rod rings made of thin wire.

Abbreviations

b/s	Breaking strain
DT	Double-taper
EFS	Extra-fast-sink
F	Floating
FOE	Figure-of-eight (retrieve)
FS	Fast-sink
G&H	Goddard & Henry
GRHE	Gold-ribbed Hare's Ear
HBN	Hollow braided nylon
HW	Hollow weave
LS	Long-shank
MS	Medium-sink
ND	Neutral-density
ST	Shooting-taper or shooting-head
WF	Weight-forward or forward-taper

Index